The Shell Guide to Country Museums

The Shell Guide to Country Museums

Kenneth Hudson

Heinemann : London

Shell UK Limited, while sponsoring this book, point out that the author is expressing his own views.

William Heinemann Ltd
10 Upper Grosvenor Street
London W1X 9PA

LONDON MELBOURNE TORONTO
JOHANNESBURG AUCKLAND

ISBN 0 434 35370 1

Designed by Jonathan Sharp
Reproduced, printed and bound by
Fakenham Press Limited, Fakenham,
Norfolk.

Contents

The Channel Islands

The East

The East Midlands

Scotland

Ulster

The Irish Republic

Introduction

THE BRITISH ISLES are fairly generously stocked with museums. There are about 1,600 of them which, in relation to the size of the population, is well above the world average. The quality, for the most part, is high, too. Museums are one of the things the British are good at.

Having said that, no harm will be done by trying to produce a working definition of a museum. One could start by saying that a museum must have some sort of permanent collection of objects, that there must be evidence of some attempt to present these objects to visitors and to interpret them, and that the museum has to have somebody in charge of it. Beyond that it is difficult to go. The museum's collection or collections can relate to any subject or any period in history. Cookery is as valid and as worthy of study and as likely to produce enjoyment as Chinese porcelain, and palaeolithic tools can be as well or as badly displayed as pop art.

An exhibition, however, is not a museum, although a museum may well contain exhibitions. The difference is one of duration; a museum goes on year after year, but an exhibition is usually a temporary affair. If everything in the Motor Show, or even a part of it, were to be preserved as a permanent collection, the result would be a Museum of the Automobile. If the same were done to the contestants for the Miss World competition, one would have a Museum of Human Anthropology. As things stand, however, both the Motor Show and Miss World are essentially exhibitions, not museums. They are transitory, they come and go.

It is perfectly true, of course, that the idea of what is and is not a museum has changed enormously during the present century. In 1900 it was almost impossible to imagine a museum without glass cases or one in which people were being deliberately entertained. The atmosphere was always serious, scholarly and reverent. Museum-going, like church-going, was not something to be undertaken lightly. But times are different, and nowadays museums know very well that they operate in a competitive market, in which the goods they have to offer must not only be good but look good. The public, unlike the profession, makes no clear distinction between an exhibition and a museum – why should it? – and finds what is offered either interesting or not interesting. The museums which acquire a reputation for being interesting are sought out and well patronised; the others are likely to be left wondering where all the people have got to.

But interesting does not mean showy or circus-like. Two of the most successful museums in Britain, measured by the number of visitors per square foot, are Jane Austen's house at Chawton, in Hampshire, and Wordsworth's cottage at Grasmere. Both are among the quietest and most restrained. The National Motor Museum at

Beaulieu, on the other hand, uses the full repertoire of the showman's tricks to make itself known and to draw in visitors from as broad a social band as possible. St. Paul's Cathedral, which employs no gimmicks at all, is equally successful. It attracts the public merely by existing and by its associations with the great. One day the Dean and Chapter may come to realise, as the owners of Longleat did many years ago, that those who should pay for the upkeep of an historic building are those who wear out its steps and floors as tourists, and at that moment the great English cathedrals will acknowledge openly that they are in the museum business and begin to see their financial problems disappear. Norwich Cathedral, by its imaginative, dignified and highly practical signposting and labelling, unequalled among English cathedrals, has already taken the important first step of presenting and interpreting the great building in its care. The next stage, of expecting those who visit the Cathedral for purely secular purposes to make a substantial contribution towards its maintenance, cannot be far off. It seems illogical and unfair that Canterbury and Salisbury should be placed, in this respect, in a less favourable position than, say, Blenheim or Stonehenge.

Museums, then, are of many kinds and many sizes. There are open-air museums, with contents ranging from old barns and blacksmiths' shops to blast-furnaces and lengths of tramway moved to the site; birthplace museums; where-the-great-man-spent-his-last-years museums; site museums, where the public can inspect the ruins of a Roman villa or an ancient watermill in comfort; country house museums; museums about a town, a village or a district; museums in superannuated steam pumping stations; underground museums in coal-mines; working farm museums, where the cows are milked by hand and never a tractor is to be seen; textile museums, where the looms can be seen operating on Saturdays and Bank Holidays; costume museums; and dozens of others. In fifty years, we have moved a very long way from the Victorian concept of a museum. The emphasis is more and more on activity and on relating the collections in the museum to the world outside. The stuffed birds and animals and the pressed flowers in stiff, orderly rows have given way to dioramas, habitat groups and nature trails; the local history collections lead naturally and usefully into neighbourhood walks organised by the museum. The museum without walls, dreamt of for so long by eccentric pioneers, has now become almost the norm.

Is a country museum in the country or about the country, or both? In what way is a country museum different from any other kind of museum? Is it just a myth, an advertiser's or showbiz confidence trick, like country clothes or country music? Does it deserve a category to itself?

The pages which follow should indicate fairly quickly what one person believes a country museum to be. The *Guide* necessarily represents a personal choice. Perhaps the most honest procedure is to begin with the author himself. He spent the first twenty-one years of his life in London and thereafter has lived only in the country, in Sussex, Kent, Yorkshire and Somerset. His work has taken him all over the world looking at museums. He has lectured about them, written about them and, as a member of the Jury for both the British and the European Museum of the Year Awards, he has done his best to sort out the museums with ideas and style from those which are, at bottom, merely ill-thought out collections of objects. And, at the end of it all, he still finds great pleasure in museum-visiting and, whenever he finds himself somewhere for the first time, always gives his first priority to seeking out its museum, to find out what the place is about.

The first distinguishing characteristic of a country museum is obviously that it is not in the centre of a large town or city but the second is that it is small. It does not present the visitor with a great flight of steps up to the entrance, or with corridor after corridor and gallery after gallery. It does not bustle with uniformed attendants. It does not give the impression that the general public is admitted on suffrance and that the real business of the museum goes on somewhere else in the building behind locked doors, with roomful after roomful of earnest researchers. It opens its arms to family parties and it has no objection to people getting excited or talking in other than hushed whispers. It is not, in short, a place which draws a clear line between learning and enjoyment. The antithesis between scholarly and popular is false. If a museum is to be both popular and good, its quality must be based on sound scholarship, on a respect for accurate information. 'Country' is not another way of saying 'slipshod, amateur', just as 'urban' is not a synonym for 'professional'. A country museum, in our sense of the word, will usually reflect its own origin. Its flavour will be local, rather than national.

To qualify as a country museum, a museum's links with the district can lie far back into the past. The great achievement of the Roman Palace Museum at Fishbourne, in Sussex, is that it brings Roman Sussex alive. It shows how money talked during that period of the county's history and invites us to make comparisons with the habits and behaviour of the land-owning class today. But one cannot expect even the best museum to do everything on our behalf and, with the British climate, one really needs to visit places in the winter to get the full story. The County Museum in Taunton, for instance, has much to tell us about the Lake Village at Meare, in the fields outside Glastonbury, but a trip to Meare in December is strongly advised, in order to experience for oneself the wetness and misery of the Lake Dwellers' lives in the winter. In June, with the birds singing, the sun shining and the buttercups in flower, Meare may present the picture of an earthly paradise, but six months later it is merely sodden and a fine source of rheumatism and pneumonia. The County Museum, entirely understandably, says nothing about rheumatism and pneumonia. The visitor has to supply these gaps from his imagination and fellow-feeling.

The countryside of course, is not concerned only, or nowadays even mainly with farming. Like the urban areas, it has its transport, its schools, its bingo, its politics and its entertainments. In any case, the countryside and its suburbs shade off physically into one another. The gradual suburbanisation of Britain and the British way of life is a process which many people may regret, but which is evidently unstoppable. From a museum point of view, this has two results: many of our 'country' museums are on the way to becoming suburban museums, and a fair proportion of those museums which really are, by any definition, country museums, are required to be larger than life, in order to satisfy the pent-up nostalgia which so many, perhaps most of us feel for the traditional rural pattern, which has been swept away. One can only regret that no museum has so far shown the courage and the perceptiveness to tackle the extremely interesting and important theme of the suburbanisation of the countryside and the myths which have accompanied it. This will have to come, but it belongs to the next generation of country museums and it is not with us yet. Meanwhile, one can only record with wonder that more copies of the *Farmer's Weekly* are sold in urban areas, especially the suburbs, than in the farming districts themselves. We are, beyond doubt, a nation of frustrated peasants, whose nostrils and ears twitch at the very mention of the word, 'countryside'.

One of the most remarkable features of the post-Second World War museum scene in Britain has been the creation of working-farm museums and rural life museums, where today's visitors can see how yesterday's rural craftsmen of all kinds, on and off the land, went about their work and how they lived. These are country museums twice over, super-country museums, which are not only in the places where people most like to find them, within sight of the fields and cows, but also tell us about country life as it used to be. They are three-dimensional novels by Thomas Hardy, with a strong touch of George Sturt's *Wheelwright's Shop* and Richard Jefferies about them and they are deservedly immensely popular. For a generation which no longer wants anything to do with the old-fashioned type of history based on statesmen, wars and treaties, they represent, like industrial archaeology, a way into the past that makes sense.

It may seem both ignorant and ungrateful to compile a *Guide* of this nature with no reference to that great source of inspiration and guidance, the Museum of English Rural Life at the University of Reading. The Museum and the man who created it during the experimental and optimistic years which followed the Second World War, the recently retired Curator, Andrew Jewell, have guided, encouraged and advised most of our countryside museums which have been set up during the past 30 years. Its fine collections, its wonderful archives, its expertise and its very high standards of scholarship have given it a place of its own in the museum field. It is not included in our list, however, for one very regrettable reason. Such a high proportion of its collections is in store, as a consequence of a sadly inadequate budget, that all that is available to the general public is a very small and tantalising tip of a very large iceberg.

Two further points seem appropriate to an Introduction. The first is that we have followed that unfashionable, but surely sensible policy of taking our examples from the whole of what used to be called the British Isles. We have, in other words, included the Republic of Ireland, partly because it would have been stupid and chauvinistic not to have done so, but even more because museums in the Republic are enjoying a most welcome renaissance at the present time and it seemed a pity not to be involved in the act.

The second point to emphasise is that, in making our selection of museums, we have done our best to cover Ireland, Scotland, Wales and England as a whole, and to keep a good balance between one region and another. There are bound to be those museums and areas which will feel a little disgruntled at having been left out, and to them all we can say is that there has been no intention of producing a museum version of the *Guide Michelin* or *The Good Food Guide* – our list contains no gradings and no stars – and that our main purpose has been to show the remarkable range of small museums which exists today. The more people go exploring on their own as a result of using this *Guide*, the happier we shall be.

As in the case of *The Good Food Guide* – the only comparison between ourselves and that prestigious and influential work – suggestions and criticisms will be most gratefully received.

A Note on the Arrangement and Details

Each museum is listed alphabetically by town within the region to which is belongs. Its name is followed by that of the body which owns and administers it.

The address of the museum should prove to be sufficiently detailed to allow most visitors to find their way without undue difficulty. It is very unlikely, however, that parking will be possible close to the entrance, especially in town centres, and the best advice one can give is 'Find a public car park and walk', a procedure which has the advantage of making it possible to absorb something of the surroundings before visiting the museum.

The opening times are the latest available, but, whenever possible, it is prudent to check them beforehand before making a special and possibly long journey. This is particularly the case when public holidays are involved. We know of very few museums which are open on Christmas Day, but apart from this no general rule is possible.

One might add, however, that, with one or two exceptions, museum curators are humane people, who take little pleasure in keeping genuinely interested visitors in the street. A letter or a telephone call in advance will only rarely fail to turn a 'Closed' day into an 'Open' day, or at least an 'Open' hour, especially if the eager visitors in question should happen to come from abroad. But it should be asked as a favour, rather than demanded as a right.

The Shell Guide
to
Country Museums

The South East

Bateman's. *The National Trust. Burwash, East Sussex, ½ mile south of A265, 3 miles west of Etchingham. Open March 1–May 31, October 1–31, Sa.–Th. 2–6. Also open Good F. 2–6. June 1–September 30, M.–Th. 11–6; Sa., Su. 2–6.*

The Wealden iron industry, active during the Roman occupation and revived in Tudor times, reached its peak during the early 17th century and many beautiful houses were built by the successful iron-masters at this time. Burwash had two forges and in 1634 the owner of one of them built Bateman's. After many years of neglect, it was bought in the 1890s by an artist and architect, who restored it and in 1902 the estate became the property of the writer, Rudyard Kipling, who did a great deal to improve both the house and the garden. On her death in 1939, Mrs. Kipling left Bateman's to the National Trust.

Many of the rooms in the house remain as they were in Kipling's lifetime. His study in particular remains exactly as he left it in 1936, with his books, chair, outsize wastepaper basket, blocks of the 'large off-white blue sheets' on which he wrote and his gadget-loaded work-table, 'ten feet long from North to South and badly congested'.

Within the park adjoining the gardens is Park Mill, a watermill dating from about 1750, although there was almost certainly a much earlier mill on the site. This is the mill which figures so prominently in *Puck of Pook's Hill* and Kipling's other Sussex stories and he took a great interest in it, especially in its practical possibilities.

The waterwheel was removed and replaced by a turbine, which drove a generator and provided electricity for Bateman's for twenty-five years. It was a considerable undertaking. From the generator and switchboard, electric current was taken 250 yards by underground cable to storage batteries in an out-building at the house. There were fifty lead batteries in open gallon-size glass containers, connected in series. It is esti-mated that their total weight was about three-quarters of a ton. Such was the cost and complexity of having a reliable, steady electricity supply in the country in the days before the grid arrived to join Burwash to the mains.

The mill was last used for grinding corn in 1902 and by 1970, when the National Trust decided to restore it, both the machines and the building were in a derelict condition. The site was over-grown and the waterways choked with weeds and rubbish. The daunting task of putting everything back into proper order, including fitting a new waterwheel, was carried out by voluntary labour, while the turbine-generator was overhauled and rebuilt by men from the Royal Engineers. The achievement received a Civic Trust award in association with the United Kingdom Council for European Archi-tectural Heritage Year in 1975.

Farnham Museum. *Waverley District Council. 38 West Street, Farnham, Surrey. Open Tu.–Sa. 11–1, 2–5; Su. 2.30–5. 'We are usually closed for two or three days before Christmas'.*

Farnham Museum, also known as Willmer House Museum, illustrates life as it has been in the past in an English

market town of considerable antiquity – Farnham first appears in the records in AD 688. The Museum is fortunate in its

Kipling's Study, left as it was during his lifetime. Bateman's, Burwash.

building, an early Georgian house, with a quiet walled garden.

Farnham is in the middle of some of England's finest hop-growing country. In the 18th and 19th centuries, Farnham hops consistently fetched the highest prices, due partly to their quality and partly to enterprising marketing techniques. The Museum makes quite a feature of hops, with photographs of hopping in the 19th century, a number of the stamps used to put particulars of the grower on hop pockets – the tall sacks into which the dried hops were pressed – tools used in the hop gardens and the kilns and bottles from local breweries.

Farnham Museum is the fortunate possessor of the John Henry Knight archive, a very fine collection of photographs of farming and country life in the late 19th century. It happens, too, to be located in the town where William Cobbett, the author of *Rural Rides* and champion of British farmers and farm workers, was born, and it has a number of

*Loom in the Local Industries Gallery.
Farnham Museum, Surrey.*

his personal effects, included in an exhibit
about him.

The timber roof structure of Westmin-
ster Hall was pre-fabricated in Farnham
in 1394-5 and the Museum is able to
display some of this woodwork, removed
and treasured when the roof was being
restored. Other interesting items in the
collections include a Georgian dolls'
house and a number of models of industrial and commercial buildings in the
district – kilns, mills, the Market House
and others.

This is a pleasant museum for brows-
ing, with more of a Georgian than a
Victorian flavour about it, which is a rare
treat among local museums.

*1754 Fire-engine. Farnham Museum,
Surrey.*

Opposite:
*Mid 19th century fire-fighting equipment.
Guildford.*

Guildford Museum. *Guildford Borough Council. Castle Arch, Guildford, Surrey. Open M.–Sa. 11–5, 'excluding Good Friday and a few days over Christmas'.*

The Museum at Castle Arch has a long history. It was established there in 1898 by the Surrey Archaeological Society and, after functioning for a number of years as the joint responsibility of the Society and Guildford Corporation, it became the sole responsibility of the local authority, although the Society still has its headquarters on the premises.

The Museum has been enlarged more than once by taking in adjacent buildings, but the original premises in Castle Arch are interesting in their own right. One of the best features is a carved fireplace of 1630, made of clunch, the hard chalk

quarried in underground workings below the Castle grounds.

The collections mainly represent the local history and archaeology of Surrey, with rather more items coming from Guildford and West Surrey than from other parts of the county. The Museum holds a large collection of Roman material, chiefly from excavated villas, although there are some interesting finds from pottery and tile-making sites.

Glassmaking and ironworking were both established in Surrey in the Middle Ages. Ironworking, which flourished here until the 18th century, has a room to itself

in the Museum, with examples of domestic ironware, cast and wrought ironwork and blacksmith's work, with exhibits explaining the processes involved. This room also contains a few relics of the very early Surrey Iron Railway, which opened in 1802.

For the 19th century, the range of exhibits is so wide that one can do little more than indulge one's fancy. A leading place should certainly be given, however, to the carefully built up and representative collection of British and foreign needlework, from the 17th century to the present day, and to the large collection of household objects gathered together by Gertrude Jekyll in the late 19th century from cottages and farmhouses in south-west Surrey. In more recent years, the Museum has extended this part of its collections by adding a wider range of rural and agricultural items, including a considerable number of craftsmen's tools.

Particular efforts have been made to collect material illustrating the industrial, commercial and social life of Guildford. This includes such things as trade cards and letter headings, theatre posters, notices of public meetings and lectures, shop fittings and the smaller types of machine, such as the cartridge-making equipment of Jefferys, the Guildford gunmakers.

One of the few famous people commemorated in the Museum is Lewis Carroll (Charles Lutwidge Dodgson). In 1868 he leased The Chestnuts, a house close to the Museum, and died there in 1898, while on vacation from Oxford. Memorabilia of Dodgson and his brothers and sisters have been deposited at Guildford and some of them are on display. They include photographs, one of his sketch books and a number of toys belonging to the family.

Wye College Agricultural Museum. *Wye College, University of London. Brook, near Ashford, Kent. The village of Brook is 3 miles south of Wye, off the A28, Ashford to Canterbury road. Open May–September W. 2–5 and August also Sa. 2–5. Parties at other times by appointment.*

A century ago about 20 per cent of the labour force in Britain was employed in agriculture, compared with eight per cent fifty years ago and two per cent today, a remarkable change for which the exhibits in the Museum help to provide a reason. The collections illustrate the gradual replacement of manual operations by machines of increasing complexity, the increasing use of iron in place of wood, the replacement of the horse by the tractor and the declining importance of the blacksmith to the farmer as the working horse disappeared and as steel and cast iron took the place of wrought iron. Most of the items in the Museum were made during the past hundred years, although some

are probably much older and many have little difference in design from similar implements used generations earlier.

The displays are housed in a fourteenth century barn and an early nineteenth century oast. Both buildings are fine examples and well worth studying in their own right. In the barn, the exhibits are grouped in bays, according to their purpose. The horse and ox trappings include the harness of the last horse to work on the College farm and in the section devoted to dairy equipment there is a Hinman milking machine of 1920. There is a good collection of ploughs and harrows. Among the exhibits are two wooden Kent ploughs, one a massive implement

Agricultural Museum, Wye College, Kent.

fitted with a broadshare, and a breast plough for cutting turf. The small donkey plough was made at the forge at Upper Hardres in about 1900 and was regularly used by a schoolmaster on his smallholding at Dunkirk until 1936.

There is a Suffolk corn drill made in 1850, of a type not very different from the machines made today, and a Massey Harris reaper-binder of 1896, one of the earliest models manufactured by this firm. The interesting range of smaller equipment includes winnowing machines, chaff cutters, potato and seed riddles, bean mills, a bone crusher, and an enormous land-measuring wheel, 5½ feet in diameter.

The oast is largely devoted to displays illustrating the growing and processing of hops. A photographic exhibition explains the work involved and this is backed up by a comprehensive collection of tools and implements, including two hop-washing machines and a hop-press, used for pressing the dried hops into the giant sacks known as pockets, and in this way making it easier to store and transport them.

The heavy cost involved in the depreciation of equipment, a great and increasing burden for farmers today, was unknown to a simpler age, before mechanical power. As this very attractive and well planned museum shows, much of the old equipment was made to last for generations. It was constantly repaired and modified and the hand tools here show considerable individual variations, suggesting that each man adapted his tools to his own particular way of carrying out his craft skill. They were, in a very real sense, an extension of himself. The machine is not so obliging or flexible.

The South

The Curtis Museum. *Hampshire County Museum Service. High Street, Alton, Hampshire. Open M.–Sa. 10–5 and Bank Holidays, except 26 December and 1 January.*

Alton is a brewing town and the present museum was built in 1870 as a result of a donation of land and money by two Alton brewers. The beginnings of the museum, however, were a good deal earlier. In 1837 Dr. William Curtis, who belonged to a well-known local Quaker family, founded the Alton Mechanics' Institute. In 1854 the Institute arranged The Alton Exhibition of Works of Art and Industry and Natural Objects. This was a great success and led to the establishment of the Curtis Museum in the following year. It continued as a privately owned and run institution until 1945, when it was transferred to the County Council.

The Curtis family connection ended in 1957 with the death of William Hugh Curtis, who became Honorary Curator in 1925, but the Museum displays contain a certain amount of material relating to the family. The gallery devoted to the natural history and geology of the area has a section devoted to William Curtis, the botanist and Fellow of the Linnaean Society. In this display there are some of the bones of that extinct bird, the Dodo, which were presented to Curtis, a somewhat surprising gift to be made to a botanist. William Curtis was the cousin of his namesake, the founder of the Museum.

Brewing became important in Alton in the 18th century, and its breweries are still a prominent feature of the town's skyline, although the small family enterprises have long since been merged into a single large national concern. The Museum tells us about the ups and downs, mostly ups, of the industry over the past two hundred years – the quality and abundance of the local water have kept it firmly rooted in Alton – and adds some details of the leading personalities associated with it. It is doubtful, however, if the sections on the town's civic and industrial history, admirable as they may be in themselves, are as popular with visitors as the small display devoted to the murder in 1815 of Fanny Adams, who was a local girl and in all probability Alton's best-known citizen.

The Museum has a considerable collection of the tools used by craftsmen and farm workers during the day when most jobs were carried out by hand, but it is also the fortunate possessor of a large number of drawings by W.H. Allen, showing these tools being used. Allen, who was born in 1863, had close family connections with Alton and when he died in 1943 be bequeathed a large number of his pictures, together with most of his collection of bygones, to the Museum. The Studies in Rural Life and Nature, as the Museum calls them, were made in watercolour, crayon, pen-and-ink and pencil. They record various forms of craftsmanship on the land and in the workshop which have been superseded by modern methods and they provide a pleasant and useful background to the displays of objects in the Museum. For many years they were shown more or less throughout the galleries, but recently they have been brought together in a new annexe, the Allen Gallery, which is about two hundred yards from the main Museum building. At the back of it is a pleasant little garden. It is the only public garden in Alton, a fact which, in a town with such a soundly based economy, can hardly be seen as a matter for self-congratulation.

Opposite:
Rural industry and crafts. Curtis Museum, Alton, Hampshire.

THE SHOEMAKER

MILLSTONE
DRESSER

Bignor Roman Villa Museum. *Privately owned. Bignor, Pulborough, West Sussex. Open March 1–October 31, Tu.–Su., 10–5.*

'The Museum,' says its proprietor, 'contains everything that has been found since the Villa was discovered by my great, great grandfather in 1811.' Among these exhibits are some of the finest mosaic floors in the former Roman world. It is probably the mosaics, rather than anything else, which attract a regular 50,000 visitors a year to Bignor, from seventy to eighty different countries.

'Villa', with its suburban overtones, is a misleading term for what were in fact the buildings of a self-contained country estate, a Roman or Romanised gentleman's rural mansion-cum-home farm. In its time a Roman villa was as functional a part of the English countryside as Holkham was in the 18th century and in both periods the well-to-do owners naturally equipped their houses with such

Mosaic Head of Venus. Bignor Roman Villa Museum, West Sussex.

amenities as the age allowed, for the comfort of themselves and their guests.

Bignor was one of the largest courtyard houses in Roman Britain. It was the centre of an estate estimated to have extended to about 2,000 acres. The buildings, including the servants' quarters, stables and other outbuildings were of stone. They seem to have fallen into decay at the end of the fourth century or beginning of the fifth. All the farmworkers and craftsmen employed, lived on the premises.

It was evidently the home of a prosperous family, with the money to decorate it with exceptionally costly mosaics. In the present museum the mosaics are displayed in their original settings. One of the most elaborate is in the Triclinium or dining-room for use in the wintertime. Several of the rooms were heated by a hypocaust system and there was a range of hot and cold baths of the type that was usual in big country houses of the period.

The site has been fully excavated and visitors can follow the layout both on the outline marked on the ground and on the model constructed to show what the estate buildings probably looked like when they were in full working order. It has been possible to calculate the number of animals for which shelter was provided. There were, it was reckoned, 200 sheep, 24 oxen and 54 head of cattle, which gives some idea of the scale of the enterprise.

The detective work on the site has been thorough. One little building in the stable block had its north end enclosed, with an apsidal end wall. This, it was thought, may have been used as a prayer room by farm servants or, in the more eye-catching phrase preferred by the Museum, by slaves. It is a nice thought.

Beaulieu Abbey: Exhibition of Monastic Life. *Lord Montagu of Beaulieu. Brockenhurst, Hampshire. Open daily Easter–September 30, 10–6; October 1– Easter, 10–5.*

The Cistercian Abbey of Beaulieu was founded in 1204. Much of it was destroyed after the Dissolution of the Monasteries – the stone went for the most part to build fortresses along the Solent – but some of the buildings have survived to the present day. They are the Refectory, now Beaulieu Parish Church; the Domus, where the Lay Brothers were accommodated; and the Great Gatehouse, subsequently remodelled and extended to form Palace House, now the home of Lord Montagu.

In 1977, on the 25th anniversary of the opening of Beaulieu to the public, a permanent exhibition, 'Monastic Life at Beaulieu', was opened in the Cellarium below the Domus. It has two aims, to help the visitor to understand the daily life of a Cistercian monk, and to tell the story of Beaulieu, explaining its relationship with other Cistercian monasteries; its involvement, through its powerful Abbots, with the political life of the times; and its place in agriculture and commerce.

The displays, which include dioramas, graphic panels, models and murals, cover every aspect of a monk's life at Beaulieu and show how his waking hours were divided between worship, work, private prayer and study. 'Work' could be of several kinds – in the cultivated plots in the Abbey precinct, in the fields at harvest time, administration, supervision of the workshops, copying manuscripts or instructing novice monks. The Cistercians based their agricultural production on units called granges. These were

*Exhibition of Monastic Life. Beaulieu
Abbey, Brockenhurst.*

farmed by lay brothers, with some hired
labour, the supervision being carried out
of previously uncultivated land and each
was organised as a separate economic
unit. In 1269 about half the 8,600 acre
Beaulieu estate was under cultivation, a
remarkable achievement for the time.
Wool was the most important source of
revenue; in 1269 there were about 4,000
sheep on the Abbey granges.

The Exhibition relies a great deal for its
information on an exceptionally detailed
Abbey account book, which was kept for
the years 1269 and 1270, and is now in the
British Library. It shows a flourishing
active community, very different from the
one that existed at the time of the Dissolution. In 1500 there were fewer than thirty

monks, the lay brothers had disappeared
altogether and most of the land was let to
tenant farmers.

Visitors to the Exhibition can follow the
story of the Abbey's rise and fall right
through to the end in 1538, when the last
Abbot was comfortably pensioned off and
the Earl of Southampton was able to
acquire the property for £1,350 6s. 8d.
After four centuries, the estate remains in
the same family. The present Lord
Montagu is a direct descendant of the
Tudor Earl of Southampton.

Buckler's Hard Maritime Museum. *Lord Montagu of Beaulieu. Buckler's Hard, Hampshire. Open every day, Easter–Spring Bank Holiday, 10–6; Spring Bank Holiday–September 30, 10–9; October 1–Easter, 10–4.30.*

Buckler's Hard lies by the side of the Beaulieu River, on the Beaulieu Manor estate. It was the brainchild of John, 2nd Duke of Montagu, who needed somewhere convenient to refine the sugar from his proposed West Indian plantations, which were never in fact established. The village was, however, built – work on it started in 1724 – but its inhabitants eventually got their living from shipbuilding, timber-processing and agriculture, not sugar.

It was very suitable for shipbuilding, sheltered from the prevailing westerly winds, and with a good depth of water in the river and plentiful supplies of timber from the Beaulieu Estate and the New Forest. More than fifty naval vessels and many more merchant vessels were built and launched here during the 18th and 19th centuries. They included Nelson's favourite warship, the *Agamemnon*.

The whole of Buckler's Hard is really an open-air museum. It has changed very little since Nelson's ships were built there. Three of the buildings are open to visitors, a small chapel, which was once a cobbler's shop; the former home of Henry Adams, the master shipbuilder, now the Master Builder's House Hotel; and the New Inn, now forms part of the present Maritime Museum, established to tell the story of the village and the river. Most of the exhibits concern events in the 18th century, when Buckler's Hard was at the height of its importance. They range from Nelson's baby clothes to a recruiting poster for HMS *Beaulieu*, one of the frigates built at Buckler's Hard during the Napoleonic Wars. A scale model of the village as it was in 1803 shows *Euryalus* ready for launching and the builders at work on *Swiftsure*, the stacks of local and

Buckler's Hard Maritime Museum.

Buckler's Hard Maritime Museum, Buckler's Hard, Hampshire.

imported timber, the sawpit, the mould loft and the blacksmith's shop.

Buckler's Hard means especially the Adams family, which built ships here for more than a century – they eventually went bankrupt as a result of trying to build too many big ships at once – and the Museum makes much of them, particularly the great Henry Adams, who is commemorated by many drawings and models of his ships. The model of the *Illustrious*, like many others in the collection, was made at the Museum by the Curator, whom visitors can often see at work at his hobby. By using Adams's own drawings, extreme accuracy to detail is possible.

The Museum is not wholly concerned with the days of the Adams. Sir Francis Chichester kept his boats on the Beaulieu River and sailed from here, and there is a display which concentrates on his exploits.

Jane Austen's House, Chawton. *Jane Austen Memorial Trust. Chawton, near Alton, Hampshire. Open April 1–October 31, daily 11–4.30. November 1–March 31, W.–Su. 11–4.30.*

Very few people would have heard of Chawton in all probability, if Jane Austen had not lived there. As it is, the six-bedroomed Chawton House has become one of the most celebrated and visited literary shrines in Britain, with a steady 30–40,000 pilgrims a year, mostly during the six holiday months. No small place can receive an annual invasion on this scale without being to some extent influenced by it.

Jane Austen's father, the Rev. George Austen, died in 1805 and after a short time his widow decided to live at Chawton, together with her two daughters, Cassandra and Jane, and Martha Lloyd. Some building work was carried out, mainly to provide greater seclusion – the Winchester Road runs along the front of the house – and considerable trouble was taken to lay out the garden attractively. Old Mrs. Austen worked a great deal in the garden until the end of her days, often picturesquely dressed in a green smock frock. An oak tree planted by Jane Austen in 1809 has been piously preserved, and the garden has been restored to what its condition is believed to have been when the Austens lived at Chawton.

After Cassandra's death in 1845, the house was divided into three dwellings for agricultural labourers. The Trustees have done their best to convert it back to its original appearance and internal arrangement and to furnish it in a way that provides an atmosphere similar to that which Jane Austen knew. There is some family furniture, including Jane's own writing table and needlework table, some

Jane Austen's House. The Drawing Room at Chawton.

of her music – she began every day with piano practice – and a patchwork quilt made by her and her mother. There is also the cup-and-ball, with which she was a skilled player, and, in the washhouse across the yard from the house, Jane's donkey cart which she used for moving about the countryside.

Chawton belongs to the most fruitful period of Jane Austen's literary life, from 1809 to 1817. Every effort has been made to show it as her home, rather than as a museum, but there has inevitably had to be some compromise, since she wrote here as well as lived here, and, without a fair ration of literary mementoes, the average visitor would certainly feel a little cheated.

The Roman Palace and Museum. *Sussex Archaeological Trust. Salthill Road, Fishbourne, near Chichester, West Sussex. Open daily, March 1–April 30, 10–5; May 1–September 30, 10–6; October 1–31, 10–5; November 1–30, 10–4.*

The Fishbourne site lies at the head of the most easterly inlet of Chichester Harbour, about a mile west of Chichester. On it are the remains of the largest Roman residence yet discovered in Britain and the only one built in a thoroughgoing Italian style. The existence of the Palace was revealed in 1960 by workmen laying a watermain. Excavations were carried out between 1961 and 1968 and as a result a great deal more is now known about the Roman conquest of Britain and the years immediately following it. The Museum puts the Palace into its historical context and tells the story of the site from its beginnings as a Roman military base in AD43 until the final destruction by fire in about AD280. All the important finds recovered from the excavations are on display in the Museum.

The Emperor Claudius invaded Britain in AD43, bringing his first wave of troops in through the safe sheltered harbour at Fishbourne. Immediately after the invasion, a group of tiled wooden buildings was constructed at Fishbourne to store the grain and other supplies needed by the army as it moved on to conquer Wessex. By AD47 most of south-east Britain had been conquered and the base at Fishbourne was no longer needed. The army had left behind, however, a good road system leading away from the harbour and much-improved port instal-

Opposite, above:
Kipling's home 1902-1936, front view and Pook's Hill. Bateman's, Burwash, East Sussex.

Opposite, below:
Wye College Agricultural Museum, Kent.

lations. The market town of Chichester quickly developed from these beginnings.

Towards the end of the Sixties construction of a large palace began on the site of the former military base. The work was completed in the early Eighties, by which time the buildings covered an area of ten acres. Four wings enclosed a rectangular courtyard garden and there was a terraced garden between the South Wing of the Palace and the deep water channel in the harbour. The natural soil was poor and the gardeners could only get plants to grow by planting them in trenches filled with specially prepared loam.

The scale of the buildings and the high quality of the workmanship, especially the marble work and the many sumptuous mosaic floors, shows that the Palace was built for someone of unusual wealth and importance. The most likely person is the local king, Cogidubnus, who was well thought of by the Romans and seems to have benefited from the conquest.

Most of the South Wing lies underneath the A27 main road and motorists should drive over it with respect. The remains of the East and West wings have been excavated and temporarily covered over again with soil. The North Wing, however, which adjoins the Museum, is protected by a shelter, so that visitors can see the walls and floors exactly as they were revealed by the excavations.

The Oates Memorial Library and Museum and the Gilbert White Museum. *The Oates Memorial Trust. 'The Wakes', High Street, Selborne, Alton, Hampshire. Open March 1–October 31, Tu.–Su. and Bank Holidays, 12–5.30.*

'The Wakes' was the home for most of his life of the Rev. Gilbert White, the 18th century clergyman-naturalist. His classic work, *The Natural History of Selborne*, was written in the house. In 1954 a public appeal for funds to buy 'The Wakes' as a memorial to White was only moderately successful, but fortunately substantial funds were made available by Mr. Robert Washington Oates, a cousin of Captain Oates, the Polar explorer, and the house was restored, redecorated and opened as a museum. The collections are in two parts, one relating to Gilbert White and Selborne and the other to the Oates

Opposite, above:
Beaulieu Abbey, Brockenhurst, Hampshire.

Opposite, below:
Exterior of Jane Austen's House, Chawton, Hampshire.

family. The first are on the ground floor, which includes the original part of the house, and the second is in the 19th century wing and mainly upstairs.

The original house, the home of a Mr. Wake, was built in the early 17th century. Gilbert White went to live there when he was nine and died there at the age of 73. He created the garden at 'Wakes' – this form of the name is more accurate than 'The Wakes' – and it was there and in the surrounding countryside that his observation and investigations on natural history were made. He is often claimed to be 'the father of field naturalists', because at that time most naturalists confined themselves to the study of dead plant and animal material, whereas he concerned himself with living species in their own habitat. He wrote letters to Thomas Pennant and Daines Barrington describing his observations and these formed the text of *The Natural History and Antiqui-*

The Wakes, with Gilbert White's ha-ha in the foreground, Selborne, Hampshire.

Left:
The Great Parlour. The Gilbert White Museum, Selborne.

ties of Selborne. An exhibition at 'Wakes' illustrates his scientific work and puts it within the context of its time.

In and around the house are many objects associated with him – the Great Parlour he built to entertain the numerous relations and friends who were his constant guests; one of his household expense books; the ha-ha which he and his

brothers built; and a short length of the Melon Wall, which he built to provide shelter for melons and cantaloupes. The garden remains largely as Gilbert White planned and planted it, and recently replanting has been carried out to make sure that as far as possible the flowers and shrubs in the garden are ones which White would have known.

The Oates Memorial Museum is devoted to two members of the family, Captain Lawrence Oates (1880-1912), who went with Scott on his Antarctic expedition and, after reaching the Pole, died on the return journey, and his uncle, Francis Oates (1840-75), naturalist and African explorer, and one of the first to write about Zimbabwe and Botswana in any detail.

It is ironical that, by a strange accident of finance, 'Wakes' should now contain, under the same roof, a museum to two great travellers and a museum to a man who never went abroad at all and who was well content to spend a lifetime exploring and observing what was within walking distance of his own home.

Gilbert White was, incidentally, never Vicar of Selborne, although he was Curate there from time to time. He was buried in Selborne churchyard, and there is a memorial window to him in the church. It shows St. Francis preaching to the birds.

Weald and Downland Open Air Museum. *Private, non-profit making company, limited by guarantee. Singleton, near Chichester, West Sussex. Open April 1–September 30, daily 10–5.30.*

The Museum was opened in 1971, with the aim of rescuing good examples of vernacular architecture – farmhouses and traditional buildings in villages and small towns – from destruction. The intention has been that the buildings re-erected on the 40-acre site shall show the develop-

Weald and Downland Museum, Single-ton, Chichester.

ment of traditional building from medieval times until the 19th century in the Weald and Downland area of Sussex, Kent, East Hampshire and Surrey. It also illustrates traditional crafts, especially those relating to building.

So far, twenty buildings have been re-erected by a small team of professional craftsmen helped by a larger number of volunteers. Most of the buildings are timber framed, with brick, flint or lath and plaster in-filling, but some have an entirely masonry structure. Watching craftsmen at work on them is one of the main attractions of a visit to the Museum. The buildings are all used for some museum purpose. They are not left as empty shells. The Hambrook Barn, for example, has been adapted for use as an exhibition hall, where there are displays explaining the different types of construction, the skilled crafts involved and the tools and materials used.

The first building to arrive at the Museum was a late 14th century house from Bough Beech, near Tonbridge, in Kent. It was in the middle of a new reservoir site, and it was presented to the Museum by the East Surrey Water Company, together with two other medieval houses from the same area, one of which had a privy as part of the house, a very rare survival and a sure sign of a rise in living standards. Other buildings at the Museum include a 16th century farmhouse from Pendean, four cattle sheds from various parts of West Sussex, three granaries, Titchfield Market Hall and Lurgashall Water Mill.

There are also a number of outdoor exhibits, grouped to illustrate a particular craft. The Woodland Area includes a sawpit and a stand of hazel, grown for coppicing and cut on a seven-year cycle to make hurdles and the woven wattle infill panels of timber-framed buildings. The Charcoal Burner's Camp shows how the kilns were prepared and fired and includes one of the huts built by the charcoal burners to shelter themselves at night-time. Three reconstructions, of a Saxon hut, a 14th century cottage and a Saxon hall, are all based on archaeological evidence and help to trace the development of traditional building during the centuries leading up to the period for which the Museum has its first surviving buildings.

The Museum also has a number of smaller items relating to what might be called rural technology – a wooden windpump from Pevensey; a 19th century horse gin used for pumping water; a man-operated treadwheel for fetching water up a 300-feet deep well.

Few open-air museums in any country can offer more pleasant surroundings than the Weald and Downland. And absolutely none have a better range of publications – guides, postcards, leaflets, broadsheets, cut-out models. This is a museum with great style, which has known from the beginning exactly what it was trying to do and which has never departed from its original standards. It is difficult to think how it could be improved.

Uppark. *The National Trust. 1½ miles south of South Harting, West Sussex, on B2146. Open April 1–September 30, W., Th., Su., Bank Holidays, 2–6.*

When, after Waterloo, the Duke of Wellington was offered Uppark, as a gift from a grateful nation, he regretfully turned it down, on the grounds that his horses would last no more than a couple of years if he lived on top of such a steep hill. But he would at least have had water. The problem of pumping water to consider-

Uppark, South Harting, West Sussex.   *The Saloon at Uppark. South Harting.*

able heights had been solved by Sir Edward Ford of Uppark in about 1650, for his own benefit. His invention, which employed a waterwheel, was used to improve the water supply of London a few years later.

The present house was completed at some time between 1690 and 1694. It was commissioned by the Earl of Tankerville, who could not have built it if it had not been for his grandfather's invention, which allowed a good supply of water to be brought in iron and lead pipes from St. Richard's Spring, a mile away and 350 feet below the house. The original waterwheel can still be seen in the little house beside the spring.

The house passed into the hands of the Fetherstonhaugh family in 1746 and it remained with them until 1968. It was remodelled, redecorated and refurnished by Sir Matthew Fetherstonhaugh in the 1750s, and when he had finished with it it looked much as it does today. Sir Matthew's exquisitely written account books are still kept at Uppark, covering all his expenditure, large and small. His son, Harry, kept up the practice when he inherited the estate.

Sir Harry married a beautiful fifteen-year-old girl, Emma Hart, who at that time was acting in the 18th century equivalent of a night club in London. She was ill-educated, with very rustic manners. Sir Harry soon got tired of her and sent her away to live with her grandmother. She survived very well, however. Romney painted her, Sir William Hamilton married her and Nelson loved her. In 1825, when he was over 70, Sir Harry married his head dairymaid, sent her to Paris to be educated, and lived very happily with her until his death at the age of 92.

H.G. Wells's mother was head housekeeper at Uppark for thirteen years and he himself had a great affection for the house and for its romantic history. The original furnishings are still there, but they have been partly rearranged to make room for exhibitions relating to the house and the family. A small upstairs room contains photographs, drawings, letters and personal possessions of successive owners of Uppark and Sir Harry's former bedroom is now devoted to the display of pieces from the great quantity of fine porcelain supplied to Uppark between 1750 and 1830. 'My old Bed at Up Park', the bed in which the Prince of Wales used to sleep in Sir Harry Fetherstonhaugh's time, has been carefully restored and now stands in a place of honour in the Small Drawing Room.

During her long widowhood, Sir Harry's wife, Mary Ann, was an indefatigable needlewoman, but the standard of her work was not high and she worked slowly, so that not many of Uppark's 18th and early 19th century furniture coverings were replaced in her time. Emma Hart may or may not be commemorated in the Dining Room. There is an unsubstantiated legend that the table there is the one on which she used to dance at the age of fifteen in the Temple of Aesculapius in the Adelphi.

Uppark has one of the most famous dolls' houses in Britain. It was made for Sarah Lethieullier, who became the wife of Sir Matthew Fetherstonhaugh. All the furniture and fittings are of the Queen Anne period and the tiny pieces of silver are correctly hall-marked.

National Dairy Museum. *National Dairy Council. Wellington Country Park, Stratfield Saye, Reading, Berkshire. Open March 1–October 31, daily 10–5.30, or an hour before dusk, if earlier. November 1–February 28, Sa., Su. 10–5.30, or an hour before dusk.*

The Museum was opened in 1978, on the Duke of Wellington's Stratfield Saye estate, to show how the techniques and conditions of milk production, retailing and processing have changed during the past 150 years. The first exhibits are concerned with milking methods. The animals in the cow shed are Shorthorns, which were the dominant dairy breed up to 1939. Since then, the black and white Friesian has taken the place of Shorthorns – four out of every five dairy cows in Britain are of this breed – and machine milking has become almost universal. The Museum illustrates the changes that have taken place in milking sheds, milking parlours and milking machines, in order to milk cows more quickly and hygienically. Primitive milking machines were introduced into Britain from America in

the 1860s, but they were of a very experimental nature and nothing really practical and reliable was available until the present century. The Museum's earliest example dates from about 1919.

There is a replica of a Victorian dairy, with its vat, moulds and curd cutters for making cheese, cream separators, butter churns, worktables, scales and 'Scotch hands' for shaping butter. There is also a typical Victorian dairy shop window, decorated with earthenware cream jugs, china cows and large swans used for displaying eggs. The exhibits dealing with the milk round will produce nostalgic thoughts for many visitors. The Museum shows how the milkman's transport has

National Dairy Museum, Stratfield Saye.

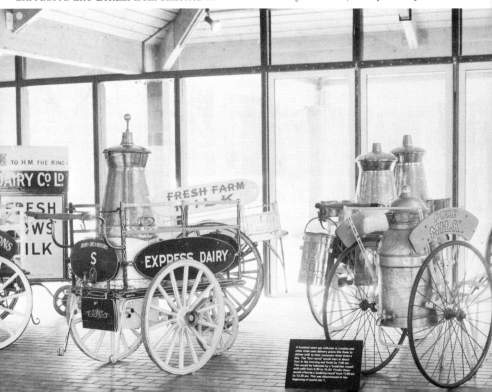

National Dairy Museum, Stratfield Saye.

developed over the years, from two pails suspended from a yoke to battery-driven electric vehicles. The Museum has examples of the different types of pram pushed by the milkman until the 1920s, when horses took over. These prams, dating from the years when there were three deliveries a day, are extremely rare survivals, although they were common enough in Victorian and Edwardian days, with their polished brass churn and an array of quart, pint and gill cans for taking the milk to the individual customer.

During the 1920s and 1930s, the churns and metal cans used on milk rounds were replaced by glass bottles. Milk bottles have changed a great deal over the past fifty years, in both design and weight, and the collection at the Museum shows how these changes have developed. There are also displays show-

ing the different methods used for getting milk from the farm to the depot over the past century – churns, horses and carts, rail tankers and road tankers. The processes involved in getting the milk from the churn or tanker to the bottle are also well illustrated. Among the items on show are examples of the laboratory, pasteurising and bottling equipment in use forty years ago, including a bottling machine which filled five bottles a minute, poor going compared with the 600 a minute which is normal today.

All this is of much technical and historical interest, with occasional nuggets of the odd and unbelievable, but for sheer charm the Museum has nothing to beat its selection from the Cow and Gate historical collection of infant feeding bottles and its display of the moulds used half a century ago in the production of chocolate animals and other creatures with strong child appeal.

The South West

The North Devon Maritime Museum. *North Devon Maritime Trust. Odun House, Odun Road, Appledore, Devon. Open Easter to September 30, Tu.–F. 11–1 and daily 2.30–5.30.*

This is a new museum, opened in 1977. It is organised and staffed entirely by volunteers, many of whom have considerable knowledge of local ships and voyaging, their fathers, grandfathers and other relatives having sailed out of Appledore years ago. The strangely named Odun House was built at the beginning of last century by a wealthy landowner who lived at Odun Hall, at the end of the road. In 1840 it became the home of the Rev. Jerome Clapp, the local Congregational minister and father of the author of *Three Men in a Boat*, Jerome K. Jerome.

The maritime history of the North Devon coast is centred on Bideford Bay and the Taw-Torridge Estuary and in this Museum, with the help of original objects and a superb collection of historical photographs, the visitor is introduced to all its

Model of Appledore Quay as it was c. 1910. North Devon Maritime Museum.

aspects – shipbuilding at Appledore, Bideford and Barnstaple, the coastal trade to South Wales to bring back coal and limestone, ocean voyages to Australia and Newfoundland, the herring industry at Clovelly, and the use of barges to bring back sand and gravel from the banks along the estuary.

The shipbuilding exhibits include a comprehensive display of the traditional shipwright's tools, with photographs of them being used to build the replicas of the *Nonsuch* and *Golden Hind*, at Hinks Yard. There is a model sawpit, showing how long lengths of plank were produced by hand labour in the days of sailing ships.

Among the many items relating to the more personal side of seafaring is a captain's sea chest, containing all his most valued possessions, including the special kind of jersey known as an Appledore Frock. These jerseys, knitted to a pattern passed down from generation to gener-

ation by word of mouth, are still made in Appledore. The room called 'The Appledore Kitchen' illustrates some of the home comforts that North Devon seamen could look forward to on their return. The picture it gives is of living conditions as they were at the beginning of this century. The equipment includes an essential item that was to be seen in nearly every household in North Devon at that time, a big pickling tub to take the stock of Clovelly herrings which carried the family through the lean period of late winter and early spring.

The Museum owns one of the boats used to catch the herrings. It is nearly a hundred years old and is now being restored, the first of a number of local boats which the Trust plans to acquire, conserve and exhibit during the next few years.

Camden Works Museum. *Bath Industrial History Trust. Julian Road, Bath, Avon. Open Sa.–Th. 2–5.*

The Museum houses the entire stock-in-trade of J.B. Bowler, a Victorian brass founder, general engineer and aerated water manufacturer, who set up in Bath in 1872. During almost a century of trading, practically nothing was thrown away, so that visitors have the opportunity of seeing a unique collection of hand tools, lathes, bottles and bottling machinery, carbonating plant, labels, invoices, catalogues, ironmonger's stock, foundry patterns and dozens of other items relating to every aspect of the firm's activity. Everything is displayed in settings that recall as closely as possible the original premises in Corn Street, which were demolished in 1972 to make room for a car park.

The Museum building itself has an interesting history. It was built as a Real

Camden Works Museum, Bath.

Tennis Court in 1777 and since then it has been at various times a malt-house, pin factory, charity school, light engineering works and luggage factory.

It is only very rarely that a collection like this is preserved in its entirety, showing exactly how such a business functioned and how it fitted into the life of the community. That community, in the case of Bowler's, extended over a surprisingly large area. The firm specialised in making and repairing the equipment used by brewers, public houses and mineral-water manufacturers and combined this with a wide range of work for local tradesmen, public institutions, such as hospitals and workhouses, farmers and private domestic customers. The staff made their rounds in a pony and trap or horse and cart, according to the size and character of the job in hand, and they often travelled considerable distances, within a radius of about 20 miles from Bath, in the course of a week's work.

It was an age in which, when something wore out or broke, a firm in one's own district was at hand to put it right, to make a new part or repair the old one. The idea of manufacturer's spares had not yet entered the industrial or commercial world.

And in a small, compact place like Bath, where the fields began only a short distance from the centre of the city, there was no real difference between town and country. Bowlers owned fields where their horses could graze and where hay was made in the summer, with the whole family lending a hand. Their customers were as likely to be farmers or village publicans as shopkeepers, peers or retired generals in Bath.

The James Countryside Museum. *Rolle Estate. Bicton, East Budleigh, Devon. Open March 24–May 24, daily 2–6 (Easter weekend 11–6); May 25– September 15, daily 10–6; September 16–September 30, daily 11–6; October 1– October 15, daily 2–6.*

Bicton House, the seat of the Rolle/ Clinton family, was sold to Devon County Council in 1957 to be used as an agricultural and horticultural training college, but the gardens and the pinetum were retained. The gardens had been neglected since 1935, but in 1961 the decision was taken to restore them to their former state and open them to the public and in 1968 a Countryside Museum was added. Much of the work involved in planning and organising the Museum was carried out by N.D.G. James, who was Land Agent to the Clinton Devon Estates for fifteen years, up to his retirement in 1976 and at that time the Museum was renamed the James Countryside Museum.

The aim has been to illustrate the far-reaching changes in farming and life in the countryside which have been brought about by the disappearance of the horse and its replacement by the tractor and the motorcar. The Museum is in three parts. The first is concerned with a particular aspect of farming or the countryside – the farmhouse, the dairy, harvest and hay-time, seedtime, cultivating – the second with tractors and the larger implements and machinery, and the third with carts and waggons. Most of the items are from the West Country. With the exception of some of the oldest exhibits, all the largest items have been restored and repainted in their original colours – bright blues, reds, greens and yellows – which makes this one of the most visually lively museums anywhere in the British Isles. The collections

Cider press and cider making. The James Countryside Museum, Bicton.

are unusually large and comprehensive, especially in the matter of tractors and implements. The tractors include a very rare Fordson of 1917, one of the earliest to survive in this country and among the implements are a barn threshing machine of 1850, a portable threshing machine of 1890 and a hay-tedder of 1875. Given the wear and tear to which farm machinery is subjected and the intensive scrap iron drives which flourished during two World Wars, it is miraculous that such early pieces of equipment should have survived.

The subsidiary displays – Cider Making, the Saddler, the Blacksmith, the Estate and the Woods, Barn Equipment and the Barn, the Thatcher, and Ploughing – are full of interesting items. The cidermaking section contains a magnificent wooden cider press from Devon which dates from about 1800. In its massive simplicity, it rivals the ancient wine presses of the Continent. The woodland exhibits include a fine collection of saws, from pit saws and quarrymen's saws to some of the first motorised chain saws. The collection of flails has for its background a large wall print showing flail-threshing in action. 'Considerable skill was needed in using a flail', visitors are told, 'and in the hands of an inexperienced man those working with him could well suffer more than the corn', a useful corrective to the widely believed myth that all country people were born skilful.

Bridport Museum and Art Gallery. *West Dorset District Council. South Street, Bridport, Dorset. Open M.–Sa. 10.30–1. June 1–September 30, also 2.30–4.30.*

The great strength of the Museum at Bridport lies in its displays relating to the town's traditional trades of net and rope making, which provided work for considerable numbers of outworkers in the surrounding villages. Until recently, the netting and cordage of Bridport was always made largely from hemp, which was grown in the area until the middle of the 19th century. Nowadays, of course, to grow even a single plant of hemp is a punishable offence in Britain, since hemp also happens to be the source of cannabis or marijuana. All hemp used here now is imported from eastern and southern Europe, but for many purposes it has now been replaced by synthetic fibres.

The yarn and twine were nearly always made in factories, but almost all the netmaking was done by women and children working at home, either with a machine or by hand with a braiding needle. The Museum explains and illustrates all the processes involved, including the often intricate cutting and fitting of the netting to shape. This is the only museum in the British Isles where the industry is described in such detail.

Bridport was also an important centre for the manufacture of sailcloth in the 18th and early 19th centuries and the Museum has some interesting things to tell us about it. In 1793 the principal firm employed nearly 2,000 people. They were in addition to those who earned a living or part of a living from growing flax, a very labour-intensive crop. With flax, as with hemp, there was a great deal of outworking. Women were paid twopence a pound for spinning and four pounds was an average day's work.

But Bridport, which is a general museum of local history and local life, has a number of other strings to its bow – the nationally famous collection of dolls formed by Dr. Donald Osmond; a fine collection of watercolours, and recently added galleries for the natural history displays and the domestic and agricultural bygones. There are also the Romano-British artifacts from the excavations carried out at the nearby hill-fort of

18th century twine 'Jack' used in the early days of rope making. Bridport Museum and Art Gallery.

Bridport Museum and Art Gallery, Dorset.

Waddon Hill in 1959, an exhibit which helps to remind us how handily Bridport, was situated for the Phoenician traders sailing their merchant ships up from the Mediterranean and for the Roman soldiers crossing over to Britain from Gaul. It seems very likely that one or other of them brought the Mediterranean plant, hemp, from the South. The Museum makes it easier to remember that human history is all of a piece, even in rural Dorset, and that a hill fort and a woman working a netting machine both say 'Romans' to us.

Cotehele. *The National Trust. Near Calstock, Cornwall. 3 miles south of the A390 on the Cornwall bank of the Tamar. April 1–October 31, daily, including Good Friday (house only closed M., but open Bank Holiday M.), 11–6 or sunset if earlier. November 1–December 23, garden, shop, restaurant and Hall of house only, daily 11–5.*

Cotehele is a remarkably well-preserved squire's house, originally fortified in the medieval tradition and improved in the late 14th and early 15th centuries, a time when the more settled conditions established by the Tudors made it possible for the landed classes to plan a more comfortable and civilised existence for themselves.

The Edgecumbe family acquired it by marriage in 1353 and it stayed with them until 1947, when the sixth Earl, on succeeding to the estates, persuaded the Treasury to accept the Cotehele property of 1,300 acres in part payment of death duties and to transfer it to the National Trust. It was the first historic country house and estate which came to the Trust

Cotehele Quay, Calstock.

in this way. The Earl died in 1965, but the family continued to leave all the tapestries, armour and furniture in the house on loan. In 1974 these, too, were given to the Trust by the Treasury, which had accepted them in lieu of estate duty on the death of the sixth Earl.

As it now stands, with four centuries' accumulation of furniture and with the modifications made by successive generations of the Edgecumbe family in order to take advantage of new opportunities for comfort and elegance, Cotehele presents probably the longest history of domestic change and adaptation of any great house in Britain, from its near-fortress days to Victorian times. There is Sir Piers Edgecumbe's Great Hall, built in the reign of Henry VIII, with heraldic

window panels displaying the arms of the West Country families into which the Edgecumbes had married – Holland, Tremaine, Durnford, Cotterel, Raleigh, Trevanion, Carew, St. Maure, Courtenay, Fitzwalter – the Tudor kitchen with its oval oven seven feet wide and three feet high, able to cope with the requirements of a squire's large household; the plastered walls hung with Flemish tapestries ruthlessly cut to fit the spaces available for them; the 15th century chapel, with the clock installed by Sir Richard Edgecumbe in about 1489, the earliest clock in England still unaltered and in its original position.

Later centuries have their own appropriate mementoes – the Punch Room, with its Bacchic tapestries made at the Soho factory c.1700; the Old Drawing Room where George III and Queen

Charlotte were entertained in August 1789 and which still contains the two maroon velvet cushions on which their Majesties sat; the room, complete with a steel mirror, in which King Charles is reputed to have slept in 1644.

Before the railway reached Calstock, very late, in 1907, everything the district needed and produced was transported by river and the Quay at Cotehele was a busy place. When the property came to the National Trust, the Quay and its warehouses were in a sadly decayed condition.

It has since been fully restored as a joint venture with the National Maritime Museum, and a small museum telling the story of the Tamar traffic has been set up in one of the warehouses. 'Shamrock', a Tamar sailing barge, built at Calstock in 1899, has been rebuilt and re-rigged and now forms part of the museum.

In the valley to the south of the house, Cotehele Mill, the manorial watermill, has been restored to working condition, together with the huge cider press which adjoins it.

North Cornwall Museum and Gallery. *North Cornwall Museum Trust. The Clease, Camelford, Cornwall. Open April 1–September 30, daily 10.30–5.*

Sally Holden is the daughter of the long-established doctor in Delabole. When she was an art student, she developed a strong interest in museums and, since there was no museum in North Cornwall, she made up her mind to start one. Her father's special knowledge of the district and the people were a great help in discovering potential exhibits and, even more, in persuading the owners to part with them, and premises were bought, in the form of an old building of considerable character and some decrepitude which had recently ended its commercial career as an intensive poultry unit. With the help of Miss Holden's family and friends, the buildings were cleaned, repaired, painted and converted and the Museum was opened in 1974. The acquisition of material continued increasingly – many of the finest items were rescued at the eleventh hour – and in 1978 the Museum received the Pilgrim Trust Award for the best small museum of the year.

The aim has been to show the life of North Cornwall as it was between approximately 1870 and 1920. The main displays relate to Slate Quarrying, Shoemaking,

Cornish kitchen range. North Cornwall Museum, Camelford.

North Cornwall Museum and Gallery, Camelford, Cornwall.

Carpentry, the Dairy and the Household. Within these broad limits, there are a number of special collections and arrangements. Three of these are particularly impressive – the upstairs and downstairs of a Cornish cottage at the turn of the century, a collection of agricultural hand tools, some of them peculiar to the area, and a fine group of early vacuum cleaners, all disgorged by local households and some of remarkably primitive appearance.

Part of the upper floor is used as a gallery, in which regular exhibitions of the works of contemporary Cornish artists are held. The Curator attaches great importance to this. She believes it does both her and the Museum a lot of good to show an active interest in the present as well as the past. The displays at the North Cornwall Museum certainly reveal a feeling for design and appearance which is considerably above the average for small museums. There is nothing provincial about them, nothing for Cornwall to be anything but proud of. But without the imagination and prodigious efforts of one person, the Museum would not be there at all. Museums are a chancy business and many of the best of them are pure accidents.

Castle Farm Museum. *R. W. Knight. Marshfield, near Chippenham, Wiltshire. Open mid-June–mid-September, W., Sa., Su. 2–6.*

Mr. Knight farms Castle Farm. The present Castle Farmhouse and its buildings date from the late 18th century, but there is an earlier farmhouse or longhouse surviving from the second half of the 16th century. There is a rare and exceptionally complete survival of its type, largely unrestored and unmodified. It is a two-storeyed building of rubble laid in courses and it was originally thatched. Some of the thatch remains, but in recent times most of the roof was covered with galvanised sheeting. This has been left in place despite its not very pleasant appearance, because it is an essential part of the history of the farm. To remove it would be to conceal an important economic fact, that the main purpose of farming has always been to make a living. If corrugated iron had been available to the 16th century farmer, he would certainly have used it. Every age does its best with the materials that exist.

The Long House was planned as a dwelling house, the Hall end, and as a place for animals, the east end, with a central cross passage which formed the entry and divided the two ends of the building. The roof had six trusses, one of which is now missing. The first floor was reached by a ladder. The south side of the

cross passage was blocked and a wing, known as the Nag Stable, was added at some time during the 18th century.

A number of the buildings at Castle Farm – the Nag Stable, the Shepherd's House, the Coach House, the Back Kitchen, with the Granary over it, and the Dairy – are open to the public. They contain a wide selection of tools, implements and equipment used in the many crafts associated with agriculture and dairying. In the Kitchen visitors can see the original stone rubbing sink, bread oven, beer copper and wash boiler. The Shepherd's House was in use until 1920 and in it are the shepherd's stove, smocks and tools. The old Dairy has been converted into a Craft Room and Shop, with occasional demonstrations of butter-making, spinning, weaving, the making of corn dollies, pottery and basket-making. There is also a display of the tools and products of Marshfield's last hurdle maker.

The Museum buildings form part of a working farm and visitors will normally be able to see livestock in and around the farmyard.

Castle Farm Museum, Chippenham.

Dawlish Museum. *Dawlish Museum Society. The Knowle, Barton Terrace, Dawlish, Devon. Open May–September, M.–Sa. 10-12.30, 2–5; Su. 2–5.*

The main emphasis of the Museum is on the way of life of a small town which has developed over the past two centuries from an agricultural village to what was known until the 1920s as 'a select resort', and then, with the growing democratisation of British society, into what it is today, a minor summer-holiday resort. The holiday trade does not figure to any great extent in the Museum: the exhibits are primarily domestic and related to past life and events in the town.

The most popular exhibits among both residents and summer visitors, are the period rooms, with household objects of Victorian and post-Victorian vintage displayed in appropriate surroundings – a parlour, an Edwardian farm kitchen, a 1920s shop and a late Victorian girl's bedroom.

With the help of a fireplace and over-mantel from a local mansion that was demolished, the room above the Museum porch has been transformed into a parlour. The pretentious clock and vases on the mantel-shelf ape the style of a grander house, apparently with no awareness of the fact that they are completely out of scale where they are, and making the point that at the heart of the bourgeoisie was a constant wish to seem more important and better off than one really was. Dawlish was very Victorian and very bourgeois and the parlour strikes absolutely the right note. The texts, the aspidistra and the portrait of Our Gracious Queen at the time of her accession are the correct symbols of respectability and, as further evidence of

affluence, every possible vacant space is filled with bric-a-brac.

Another aspect of Dawlish is provided by the Corner Shop, where progress and conservatism are skilfully combined. The solid ornamented cash-register is an early model, imported from the United States. The shelves display a range of boxes and tins which were available at the time. This is a general store of the mid-Twenties, but there are many indications that it is a shop with years of solid prosperity behind it, with no need to indulge in brash or aggressive modernity.

Dawlish is on the edge of rural Devon, as well as the sea, and the values and aspirations of the farming class and the small town bourgeoisie were not at all the same in Victorian times. So the Museum decided to have a Farm House Kitchen, as a foil to the Parlour. This is a living kitchen, warm and homely, unlike the bleak, efficient kitchen of a great house with a retinue of servants. The kitchen range, from a house only a few hundred yards from the Museum, provides hot water, bakes, boils and warms the occupants of the settle and Windsor chair which flank it. On the mantelpiece, a pair of treasured Staffordshire dogs sit on either side of the steeple clock from Connecticut. The range is blackleaded, the brass polished, but a pair of muddy boots are not out of place, as they certainly would have been in the Victorian parlour.

Opposite, above:
Dawlish Museum, Devon.
Opposite, below:
The Corner Shop. Dawlish Museum.

Devizes Museum. *Wiltshire Archaeological and Natural History Society. Long Street, Devizes, Wiltshire. Open Tu.–Sa. 11–5.*

The Museum in Devizes is concerned chiefly with the prehistory of Wiltshire. Its collections, which are of international importance, illustrate man's struggles to achieve a state of civilisation. No other county in Britain is better provided with the sites and monuments of antiquity. The two great chalkland regions of Salisbury Plain and the Marlborough Downs, with their good natural drainage, were especially favourable to primitive communities who were introducing farming techniques into Britain for the first time.

A Society to study the history, archaeology and natural history of Wiltshire was established in 1853 and a museum was created in the same year. Today it is one of the oldest surviving institutions still administering its own notable museum and library. Much of the material from the excavations carried out on prehistoric, Roman and Saxon sites within the county during the later 19th and the present century has found its way to Devizes Museum, many of these digs having been sponsored by the Society itself. The most important items in the archaeological collections are pottery, tools, weapons, ornaments and personal finery of the period 3500 BC up to the Roman conquest, but what is preserved from later sites is also impressive.

There is a comprehensive natural history collection at the Museum. This reflects the work of the Society's very active Natural History section and consists of collections of local birds, molluscs, lepidoptera and geological specimens. There are also two herbaria.

Within the last ten years, the Society has raised large sums of money to improve and enlarge the Museum galleries

Early Bronze Age Necklace 1800-1400BC. Devizes Museum.

Opposite:
Devizes Museum, Wiltshire.

and to put its finances on a sound basis. Having survived a critical period, during which many other county societies have handed over the responsibility of their Museum to a public body, usually the County Council, the Wiltshire Society believes it has shown that a satisfactory partnership between the public and the private sector is perfectly possible and that there are very great advantages in preserving one's independence.

Devizes Museum is a lively, enthusiastic place, where the visitor can feel the presence of enterprise and new ideas and where the frustrations of bureaucracy and committees have been kept at a safe distance. It gains enormously by not being too big. Nobody goes away exhausted.

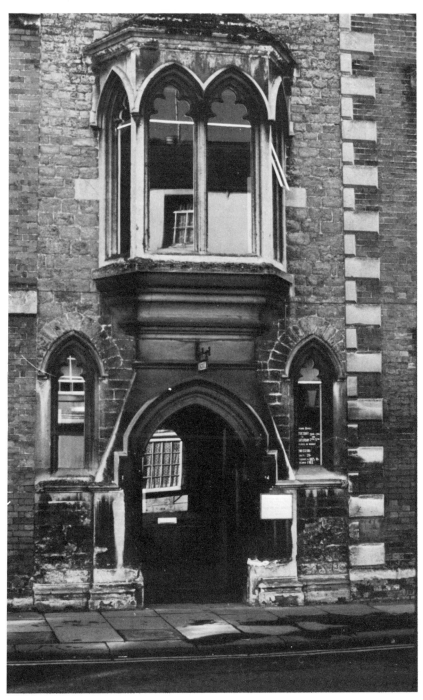

Dorset County Museum. *Dorset Natural History and Archaeological Society. High West Street, Dorchester, Dorset. Open M.–Sa. 10–5.*

The Dorset Society 'exists to promote an active interest in archaeology, natural history, geology, local history, the fine arts and similar subjects in the county of Dorset'. The Museum, which was founded in 1846, belongs to the Society. In 1883 it found a permanent home in the present building, which was erected for the purpose by public subscription. The premises were considerably extended in 1952 and again in 1970.

There are six main divisions: the Thomas Hardy and Dorset Worthies Gallery, the Archaeological Gallery, the Natural History Gallery, the Geology Room, the Temporary Exhibition Gallery and the Bygones Collection.

Thomas Hardy and the Dorset Worthies occupy most of the main Victorian Hall of the Museum, characterised by its fine cast-iron work, which has been redecorated in accordance with the original colour scheme. Both the design and colour of the ironwork were influenced by the Great Exhibition of 1851. The main exhibit here is the reconstruction of Thomas Hardy's study at Max Gate, his house near Dorchester. It contains books from his library, a large collection of his manuscripts and some of his personal possessions. Elsewhere in the hall are items of furniture belonging to Hardy, and memorabilia of the Dorset poet William Barnes, and Alfred Stevens, the Victorian artist and sculptor, and Nelson's flag captain at Trafalgar, Admiral Sir Thomas Masterman Hardy. The gallery of the main hall contains local history material from the Anglo-Saxon period onwards.

Opposite:

Roman mosaics in the Dorset County Museum (1881). Dorchester.

The Society has notable archaeological collections. They include much of the material discovered by Sir Mortimer Wheeler during his excavations at the Neolithic and Iron Age hill fort, Maiden Castle, between 1934 and 1937. The Roman period in Dorset is also well represented. The collections of the fauna and flora of the county, displayed in the Natural History Gallery, include a number of species no longer recorded in the area. The Geology Room uses murals, maps and pictures, in conjunction with rocks and fossils, to tell the story of the physical structure of Dorset over the last 195 million years. Among the exhibits are remains of the giant reptiles which lived in the region until the climate changed and creatures better adapted to the colder conditions took their place.

The Skyrme Collection of Bygones is housed in what was the coach house and stables of the George Inn, which once occupied the Museum site. It includes a wide range of items used by our grandparents and great-grandparents in the course of their daily life and especially of the tools and equipment used by craftsmen, craftswomen and tradesmen.

Tourism is one of Dorset's most important industries and the Society tries, through its Museum, to give both visitors and residents a better understanding of why this essentially rural county is what it is, and why it has a flavour of its own. In a sense, of course, the whole of Dorchester is a museum. The Old Crown Court, for instance, up the street from the County Museum, is one of the most evocative buildings in Britain, where it is almost impossible not to have a mental picture of the six Tolpuddle Martyrs standing in the dock, receiving with such dignity their savage sentence of transportation. And nearly opposite, is the house where Judge Jefferies lodged while he was in the process of handing out his even more vicious treatment to those unfortunate enough to have been involved in the Monmouth Rebellion. A few yards further on is the County Jail itself, and a final reminder of the power and severity of the law, and close to it, the statues of Thomas Hardy and William Barnes 'survey' Dorchester and all it stood for. The County Museum is a useful launching pad for explorations of this kind.

Somerset Rural Life Museum. *Somerset County Council. Abbey Farm, Chilkwell Street, Glastonbury, Somerset. Open Easter–October 31, M.–F. 10–5; Sa. 10–6; Su. 2–6. November 1–Easter, M.–F. 10–5; Sa., Su. 10–4. Evening opening by appointment.*

The Museum, opened in 1975, is arranged in Abbey Farmhouse and the adjoining Abbey Barn. The Abbey Barn was built about 1370 as the storehouse or home barn of Glastonbury Abbey. It is one of the finest barns in the country, with a magnificent timber roof structure and stone sculptures, illustrating the prosperity of the Abbey at the time it was built. It remained in use as a barn until 1972, and two years later it was given to the County Council as the centre-piece of the new Somerset Rural Life Museum. It now houses a collection of horse-drawn agricultural implements, including waggons and carts, cider-making equipment, and peat-digging tools, including a peat boat and a barrow used to carry peat on the moors of central Somerset.

Many of the exhibits in the Barn date back to Victorian times, although one or

The Abbey Barn. Somerset Rural Life Museum, Glastonbury.

two are earlier, and all come from Somerset farms. They include a barn threshing machine of 1860; a seed riddle dated 1772; a twin-screw cider-press, made c.1880; and a waggon of c.1860, used at Eastern Farm, Pedwell, by three generations of the Taylor family for transporting produce to Glastonbury and Bridgwater markets.

The Abbey Farmhouse is mostly Victorian. It has a purpose-built dairy, with a cheese room above. The adjoining cowsheds and outbuildings were added after the turn of the century. After the death of the owner in 1969, the premises were all acquired by Somerset County Council, to complete the site of the new Museum.

The two rooms on either side of the entrance hall have been used to illustrate

Farm waggon c. 1860 in the 14th century house-barn of Glastonbury Abbey, Somerset Rural Life Museum.

the life of a farmworker, John Hodges (1828-91), who lived at Butleigh, four miles from Glastonbury. The exhibition documents his career from the cradle to the grave and weaves it into the conditions of the time. The kitchen has been decorated and furnished to resemble as far as possible the kitchen of a large farmhouse in the 1890s and the dairy has equipment of the same period, including cream pans and skimmers, box and barrel butter churns and butter pats.

The Museum has a large and growing collection of photographs illustrating all aspects of rural life in Somerset and many tape-recorded reminiscences of conditions as they used to be in the early years of the present century. These include the memories of a village blacksmith, cooper and baker, a midwife, a housemaid, a teazle grower and a landowner and reflect in a personal and convincing way the activities and social relationships of the county before the traditional village structure disintegrated.

Cookworthy Museum. *William Cookworthy Museum Society. 106 Fore Street, Kingsbridge, Devon. Open from 2 weeks before Easter to mid-October, M.–Sa. 10–5. During the winter, groups are welcomed, by prior arrangement.*

The Museum is in the old Grammar School, built in 1670 by Thomas Crispin, as a token of gratitude to the town of his birth. The original panelled schoolroom, with the Headmaster's dais and canopied seat, still remains. The school was moved to other premises in 1931, after which the old buildings deteriorated rapidly. It was restored in 1971, with financial and practical assistance from English China Clays Ltd., and converted into a museum and community centre. Roughly half the present Museum is devoted to William Cookworthy and half to collections of local history, costumes and toys.

Cookworthy, born near Kingsbridge in 1705, was the first to recognise the china clay of Devon and Cornwall as the kaolin that the Chinese used in the manufacture of their porcelain. After many experiments, he pioneered English hard paste porcelain, first in Plymouth and then in Bristol. The Museum has a small collec-

Coal-fired kitchen range. Cookworthy Museum, Kingsbridge.

tion of examples of his work and there are exhibits showing the processes used in the 18th and 19th centuries to extract, refine and dry the clay and, as a striking contrast, the way the same job is done today.

The founder of the Grammar School is commemorated by a room named after him. The Crispin Room traces the history of the School and its pupils, with early documents, team and other photographs, uniforms and prizes. Adjoining this is another room which is used to display part of the local history collection. Among the exhibits here are tools and equipment relating to the traditional trades and industries of the district. The maritime section, with its tools, paintings and half-models, is a reminder that both Salcombe and Kingsbridge were shipbuilding towns in the 19th century. Until late Victorian times, the South Hams, the part of Devon surrounding Kingsbridge, was rather isolated by bad roads, so that the old way of life went on longer here than elsewhere in the county.

The school kitchen, which forms part of the Museum, has seen little change from the days when the cook catered for 60 boarders and the Headmaster's household. The huge cast-iron range was made at a Kingsbridge foundry. The wall cupboards hold the moulds, dishes, china and cutlery which were necessary for such a large establishment. The adjacent scullery has a floor of local slate, which helped to keep it cool on a busy washday. The large copper for heating the water is still in its place in the corner. There is also in this room an exhibit illustrating dairying in South Devon. It includes equipment used for making clotted cream.

Agriculture has always been the most important industry in the South Hams, and Kingsbridge is still the market town for the area. The Museum naturally devotes a good deal of space to farming, partly in its indoor exhibits and partly in a new outside gallery for large implements, the only such collection in South Devon.

Fox Talbot Museum. *The National Trust. Lacock, Wiltshire. Off the A350, 3 miles north of Melksham. Open March 1–October 31, daily 11–6. Closed only on Good Friday.*

William Henry Fox Talbot (1800-77) was a distinguished mathematician, archaeologist and classical scholar, who became a member of the Council of the Royal Society at the early age of 36. Lacock Abbey was a family property and Fox Talbot lived there from 1827 until his death. In the early 1830s, he began to use a camera lucida and camera obscura during his travels abroad, as optical aids to drawing, and started experiments aimed at retaining permanently the images reflected by these instruments. He announced his photographic process early in 1839, at almost exactly the same time as Daguerre, although the two systems were different.

For the next few years he continued his experiments, but gradually moved away from research on photography in the narrow sense and concentrated on perfecting techniques of photo-mechanical reproduction, so that photographs could be used as illustrations in books. He made important contributions to spectroscopy, electro-magnetism and the coating of metals, but the main interest of the last twenty years of his life was the translation of Assyrian cuneiform inscriptions.

The Museum illustrates the life and achievements of this many-sided man, who was fortunate enough to live in an age

Fox Talbot Museum, Lacock, Wiltshire.

of tremendous progress in the arts and the sciences, before the arrival of the narrow specialist. The large stone-built 16th century barn near the entrance to Lacock Abbey has been skilfully converted into a number of display areas, a documentation centre and an audio-visual theatre. Since the Abbey is also open to the public, visitors have to walk only a short distance in order to see where Fox Talbot lived and where he took a number of the pioneering photographs which are shown in the Museum.

Apart from its treasure-house of photographs, the Museum also has many exhibits which illustrate Fox Talbot's wide range of interests and his methods of work. There are, for example, five of his personal collection of Egyptian tablets, one of his microscopes, the medals he was awarded in acknowledgement of his scientific achievements, and two of his cameras.

The small audio-visual cinema, seating forty people, shows a slide-tape programme about Lacock Abbey and a description of his negative/positive photographic process, invented and improved while he lived there. The visitor is tempted to wonder, after seeing both the Abbey and the Museum, what kind of life Fox Talbot would have created for himself had he been born 150 or even 100 years later.

Philpot Museum. *Philpot Museum Trust. Bridge Street, Lyme Regis, Dorset. Open May 1–September 30, daily 10.30–1, 2.30–5. October 1–April 30, Th., Sa., Su. 2.30–5.*

The Museum is on Gun Cliff, overlooking the sea in the heart of the old town. It was built by the Philpot family in the early 1920s, and considerable restoration, redecoration and re-arrangement took place after the Second World War. A fair summary of the improvements would be to say that wonders have been achieved with a charming, but, from a museum curator's point of view, far from convenient building.

The ground floor is concerned mainly with local history of one kind and another, the exhibits including portraits of Lyme personalities, relics of the Monmouth Rebellion, the 13th century Borough Seat, and a copy of Jane Austen's novel, *Persuasion*, which was partly set in Lyme.

The most notable collection, however, is that of liassic fossils in the first floor gallery. The cliffs around the town represent one of the richest sources in Britain of the fossilised remains of animals, fish, reptiles and plants. The most common specimens are the ammonites and belemnites, which are easy to find in the debris at the foot of the cliffs. The star exhibit, however, is the fossilised ichthyosaurus, or fish lizard, which lived about 140 million years ago in the Age of the Great Reptiles. The first specimen of this kind was discovered in 1811 by Mary Anning, who was a native of Lyme Regis and who became famous for her geological knowledge and collecting fervour. Another gallery on the same floor contains more local history and exhibits illustrating the archaeology of West Dorset, from the Stone Age to the time of the Roman occupation. There are also collections of photographs of old Lyme, and of lace, some of it dating back to the 17th century.

By climbing an iron staircase from the Fossil Room, one reaches the Picture Gallery. This contains a collection of prints and drawings which show the town and the surrounding district from the time of Queen Elizabeth I onwards.

The smallness of the Philpot Museum is appealing. It reflects the compactness and old-fashioned quality of Lyme. Visitors seem to appreciate the quick dip it offers into the history and surroundings of this ancient town.

Portland Museum. *Weymouth and Portland Museums Service. 217 Wakeham, Portland, Dorset. Open April 1–September 30, M., W., Th., F. 10–8; Tu., Sa. 10–5; Su. 11–1, 2–5. October 1–March 31, Tu.–Sa. 10–1, 2–5.*

Portland Museum was opened in 1930. At that time, it was housed in two old cottages, 217 Wakeham and 'Avice's Cottage', on the corner of Church Ope Road. 'Avice's Cottage' took its name from the heroine of Thomas Hardy's novel, *The Well-Beloved*. Dr. Marie Stopes had lived on Portland for several years and was largely responsible for founding the Museum. She gave the two cottages for the purpose – they were in poor condition at the time – and they were restored and equipped by public subscription. In the 1970s a large extension was built at the back of the original premises, and this has doubled the area of the Museum.

Portland is an unusually interesting place and a museum based there could hardly fail to be stimulating. There were Stone Age, Bronze Age, Iron Age and Roman settlements on the island, its fortifications were important as a defence against the French in medieval and Tudor times, and it saw considerable fighting during the Civil War. It has been a naval base for a long time and it has a Borstal Institution, formerly a prison with a tough

Opposite, above:
Weald and Downland Museum, Singleton, West Sussex.

Opposite, below:
Rural Life Gallery. The James Countryside Museum, Bicton, Devon.

reputation. Its stone industry dates back to the Middle Ages and has provided material for prestigious buildings all over the world. Its fossils are exceptionally varied and attractive.

All these aspects of Portland are reflected in the Museum. 'Avice's Cottage' now accommodates Natural History, Portland Stone and, inside and outside the building, Fossils. 217 Wakeham has Ships and the Sea and general exhibits. The New Gallery looks after the History of Portland.

Like all museums, Portland has exhibits which, rightly or wrongly, command an unusual share of public interest and

Opposite, above:
Cotehele, Calstock, Cornwall.

Opposite, below:
Finch Foundry Museum, Sticklepath, Devon.

Portland Museum, Dorset.

attention. It is not difficult to make a short list of the Museum's star turns. Among the fossils, are the giant ammonite and the collection of fossils known to the old quarrymen as 'fossil crow's nests' or 'fircones'. These beautiful fossils, Cycads, are the crowns of a palm-like sub-tropical tree which is no longer found in temperate zones. An equally sure draw is the original mechanism for turning the light at Portland Lighthouse, in use from 1906 until its eventual replacement in 1976. But, such is human nature, the general favourite among visitors is the collection of objects connected with the old convict prison. This includes carvings made by the prisoners, manacles, leg-irons and, the Museum's most celebrated exhibit, a roof-slate engraved by a convict imprisoned for forgery.

Wheal Martyn Museum. *St. Austell China Clay Museum Ltd. Wheal Martyn, Carthew, St. Austell, Cornwall. On the A391 between St. Austell and Bugle, about 2 miles from St. Austell town centre. Open April 1 (or Good Friday, if earlier) – October 31, daily, including Bank Holidays, 10–6. Other months by appointment.*

China clay, or kaolin, is the result of the partial decomposition of the felspar in granite, the other constituents, mica and quartz, remaining unaltered. Deposits were discovered in Germany, France and Cornwall during the 18th century, a thousand years after the Chinese had begun to use it. So long as the pottery

Below and Opposite:
Wheal Martyn Museum, St. Austell, Cornwall.

industry remained the only customer, production was on a small scale, but with the introduction of art paper, photographic half-tone blocks, and mass circulation newspapers, the demand increased dramatically. In 1858 85 pits owned by 42 different companies produced 65,000 tons; 120 years later 26 pits owned by 5 companies produced 3 million tons.

Wheal Martyn Museum tells the story of what is now Cornwall's most important industry. The original initiative came from the English China Clays Group, the world's largest producer of china clay, but help and support have come from the whole industry. The museum site includes two old clay works. The main one, Wheal Martyn, has been restored, to show the processes as they were before the industry was transformed during the period after the Second World War, while the reception area has been built inside

the ruined remains of the Gomm Clay Works. Gomm Works began operating in 1878 and closed in the 1920s. Wheal Martyn has had a longer and more varied history. The pit and works here worked as a unit from the 1820s until 1931. The pit then closed for 40 years, but its clay is now piped down to modern works elsewhere in the area to be refined and dried. The Wheal Martyn works, however, continued in operation until 1969, processing lower grade clay from other pits in the valley.

The two parts of the Museum illustrate all the stages of china clay production as it used to be – washing the clay from the pit-face, pumping the slurry to channels known as drags, where the fine sand and the mica were removed – the coarse sand was taken out at the pit – running the refined clay slurry into settling tanks and finally drying it, ready for storage in a long building called a linhay. Eventually it was packed into bags or barrels for shipment, and the Museum tells about that, too – the 3-ton horse-drawn waggons, which had to be taken, 100 of them a day, down to the harbour at Charlestown, over very difficult roads; the 4-ton motor lorries which began to replace the horses in the 1920s; the development of the modern china-clay ports at Par and Fowey.

A number of items of equipment have been moved to Wheal Martyn from other pits and clay works, but buildings or machinery which cannot be easily moved are being treated as satellite sites. They include the china stone grinding mill at St. Stephen and the beam pumping engine at Parkandillack. It is also hoped to add before too long another satellite which visitors are certainly going to find of great interest, an example of the old type of clayworker's cottage, complete with the vegetable garden and the pig in the sty which played such a large part in maintaining the standard of living of these very hardworking and independent-spirited people, half industrial workers, half peasants.

The Barbara Hepworth Museum. *Executors of the Artist's Estate. Trewyn Studio, Barnoon Hill, St. Ives, Cornwall. Open mid-October–mid-March, M.–Sa. 10–4.30. Mid-March–June 30 and September 1–mid-October, 10–5.30. July 1–August 31, 10–6.30. Open Bank Holidays and New Year's Day.*

This is one of the very few museums in Britain to be wholly devoted to a single artist, housed in the premises where that artist lived and worked. Barbara Hepworth lived at Trewyn Studio from 1949 until her death in 1975, at the age of 72, and it was here that the greater part of her work was produced. She asked her executors to try to set up a permanent exhibition of her works in the house and in the garden and to show her studio as nearly as possible as it was in her lifetime. The studio was damaged in the fire that caused her death and much of the furniture and books cannot be exhibited. An attempt has been made, however, to recreate something of the atmosphere of Trewyn Studio in the 1950s and at the same time to present the essential features of the artist's life and career. One of the most attractive aspects of the Museum, in both the house and the garden, is its peacefulness, particularly welcome in summer, when the narrow streets of St. Ives are crowded with visitors and their cars.

The downstairs room, entered directly from the street, was originally the kitchen, dining-room and bathroom. It now contains photographs of Barbara Hepworth,

Trewyn Studio Garden with Sculptures. Barbara Hepworth Museum, St. Ives, Cornwall.

Left:
Barbara Hepworth, 1972. Barbara Hepworth Museum, St Ives, Cornwall.

taken at various stages of her career and in the five showcases, documents, memorabilia and other photographs tell the story of her life. In an alcove are her woodcarving tools and a number of unfinished wood carvings. The room on the first floor served as a workroom, bedroom and sitting room. It now contains some of the original furniture and a selection of wood and stone carvings, representing every period of her career. They include the *Infant*, modelled after her son in 1929, and *Single form* (1961), made after the death of her close friend, Dag Hammarskjöld.

The sub-tropical garden, with its 20-feet high granite walls, was Barbara Hepworth's own creation. It contains three large stone carvings made during the 1950s and a group of eighteen bronzes. In the greenhouse is her collection of cacti. On one side of the garden is the yard where she did most of her carving, the turntable exactly as it was at the time of her death, with the marble block for a multipart carving in place. The plaster and stone-carving workshops have also been left as they were in 1975.

Barbara Hepworth loved Cornwall and her work was affected by the shapes and textures of the landscape. She was the most distinguished and most permanent member of the colony of artists who moved in and out of St. Ives and the town is graced by a number of her works, sculptures in the courtyards of two blocks of flats, in the Library, outside the Guildhall, at the Cemetery, in the Parish Church and near the Railway Station. There are, in fact, two Barbara Hepworth museums in St. Ives; one in Trewyn Studio and the other in the town itself.

Shaftesbury and District Museum. *Shaftesbury and District Historical Society. Gold Hill, Shaftesbury, Dorset. Open Easter–September 30, M.–Sa. 11–5; Su. 2.30–5. Other times by appointment.*

Make no attempt to drive to the Museum. There are plenty of car parks in Shaftesbury. Leave the car in one and walk to the Museum from there. Shaftesbury is a hilltop town, with steep, narrow lanes descending to the plain that surrounds it. The Museum behind the Town Hall in the High Street, is at the top of one of these lanes and there are wonderful views from its little garden.

It is housed in a former cottage, which has been pleasantly and skilfully converted into a museum, without destroying its character. The collections, built up since 1946, reflect exactly the interests and intention of the Society which brought them into being. Anything which provides a clue to the way local people lived, worked and thought in the past qualifies for preservation and display. The result is a much-visited museum of great charm, which fully deserved its 1976 National Heritage Award.

The arrangement is, like life itself, impressionistic, rather than systematic. The past is recreated by putting a hand into the historical bran tub and looking at

The Byzant. Shaftesbury and District Museum.

Shaftesbury and District Museum, Dorset.

what comes out with one's heart as well as one's eyes – a smock and crook, animal and man traps, sheep bells, a baker's peel, a dried cat (for scaring vermin), a worsted winder, sugar cutters, butter prints, a flail, cider owls, house bells, tradesmen's paper bags, valentines, hat boxes, a pit saw, union banners, bills, a magic lantern. By the time the visitor has spent half an hour here, he will almost certainly have a feeling of what life was like in Dorset before the old, self-contained, ingenious, superstitious, hierarchical, rural society gave place, for better or worse, to the electrical, motorised, packaged culture we have today.

The collections miss nothing, disdain nothing, but there are inevitably some strong points where specialisation has occurred simply because Shaftesbury is what it is and where it is – a display devoted to Dorset buttons, at one time an important local cottage industry; lace-making; the Shaftesbury hoard of Saxon coins dug up in 1939; the town's 1744 fire engine, with its leather buckets and hose.

The oddest exhibit, or perhaps one should say the exhibit with the oddest associations, is the Shaftesbury Byzant, a strange relic, which was decorated with money and jewels and used in a ceremony to perpetuate the right to draw water from the nearby springs at Enmore Green (Shaftesbury has no natural water supply within the town itself). This was celebrated each May, when the Mayor offered the Byzant, together with a penny loaf, a calf's head, a pair of gloves and a gallon of ale to the Lord of the Manor. Dancing followed and the procession then returned to the town with the Byzant, when the revelries continued. The ceremony, one is not surprised to learn, has been recently revived.

Sherborne Museum. *Sherborne Historical Society. Abbey Gate House, Sherborne, Dorset. Open April 1–October 31, Tu.–Sa. 10.30–12.30, 3–4.30. November 1–March 31, Tu., Sa. 10–12.30, 3–4.30. March 1–November 30, Su. 3–4. December 1–February 28, Su. 3–4.30.*

Sherborne Museum was opened in 1968 to illustrate 'aspects of the history and environment of Sherborne and nothing else'. Pleasantly housed in the centre of one of Britain's most attractive market towns, it makes very full use of the limited space available in the medieval gate house. Sherborne today means mainly

Opposite:
Sherborne Museum, Dorset.

Below:
Dolls' House c. 1870. Furniture c. 1840. Sherborne Museum.

schools, shops and Abbey, and the Museum is interested in all of them to some degree, although the older the institution the more attention it receives, which is the normal way of historical societies. There are drawings to show how Sherborne Abbey, founded in 705, was reconstructed and modified at various dates and there are fragments of medieval tiles and stonework, the flotsam and jetsam thrown up by the venerable building as it moved from one period of its life to another. There are also facsimile colour reproductions of the manuscript of the splendid Sherborne Missal, made in the Abbey c.1400. Sherborne School – the boys' school – was founded as long ago as 1550 and so qualifies for its display of documents and pictures, but its sister institution, Sherborne School for Girls, as a mere Victorian foundation, has yet to receive the Museum's accolade of recognition.

Local families and notabilities are well represented, and so are the two Castles, Roger of Caen's twelfth century castle, and the New Castle, built by Sir Walter Raleigh in 1594 and still a residence. Roman Sherborne is represented through a collection of pottery and other artifacts found locally, including portions of painted plaster from a villa excavated in the area. There is a separate display of pottery of various periods from sites in and around Sherborne, together with slabs from a medieval hearth of some kind, quite possibly a pottery drying floor, which was found under the floor of a classroom in Sherborne School. This must surely have been among the most comfortable archaeological excavations ever undertaken in Britain or anywhere else, with walls, windows and a good roof to protect the diggers from the elements and electric light to enable the work to proceed day and night.

The now extinct Sherborne silk industry receives special attention – quite rightly, since for generations it was the town's main employer. The Museum's display traces its history from the seventeenth century onwards, with the invaluable help of letters and account books from William Willmot's silk mills and samples of the fabrics themselves. To round off the story, there is an exhibit devoted to the glassfibre fabrics which have been made in Sherborne since 1942. The new industry took over the premises of the old one, and was able to take advantage of the textile skills which had been handed down from family to family over a very long period.

The Natural History section puts man in his place, as just one local ecological specimen among many. There are flower paintings by a Sherborne artist, a collection of butterflies and moths found within a 15-mile radius of the town centre, a number of river and downland habitat scenes and, most appealing of all, the Diorama of Oak Ash Wood, showing the birds, beasts and insects to be found in it, sections of its tree trunks, with drawings of each tree's characteristic form, flowers and fruit. A 10-minute walk brings one out into the country from any part of Sherborne. It is a country town in the full sense of the term and its Museum emphasises the fact very pleasantly.

Finch Foundry Museum. *Finch Foundry Trust. Sticklepath, Devon. On A30, 4 miles from Okehampton. Open April 1–October 31, 11–6. November 1–March 31, 11–dusk.*

From 1814 to 1960, agricultural tools of a very high quality – scythes, hoes, bill-hooks, shovels, mattocks, axes, hooks – were made at the Foundry at Sticklepath. 'Foundry' was a misnomer, since the business carried on there by successive generations of the Finch family was that of a forge, not a foundry. It was of great importance to the village and until the outbreak of the Second World War up to twenty local men were employed there, making tools that were famous throughout the south-west of England. After the war, the demand for its products declined,

partly because of competition from mass-produced tools, but also because hand tools are less and less used on the farm as time goes on.

After the works was closed, it rapidly became derelict. The roof collapsed, leaving the machinery open to the weather, and a great deal of restoration and repair has been necessary in order to make the buildings and their equipment usable again.

The machinery was powered by water from the River Taw. A pair of trip or tilt hammers, rare survivals in the West of England, were driven, together with some ancillary machinery, by one waterwheel and a second powered a fan from which air was taken to the various forges through a

Water-powered tilt hammers and metal cutting shears. Finch Foundry Museum, Sticklepath.

system of underground pipes. A third waterwheel drove the grinding mill, where the tools were sharpened and finished. Here visitors can admire the great sandstone grinding-wheel running in water, where the operator lay face down on a bench to hold the tool against the revolving stone. His head was very close to his work, giving real meaning to what is now only a metaphor, 'nose to the grindstone'.

The complex of buildings forming the Foundry was formerly a cloth mill, which became the hammer room, and a corn mill, which was converted into the grinding house. At one time there were a dozen of these small mills along the banks of the Taw at Sticklepath. The Finch Foundry wheels are served by a leat, which brings the water from the river into a wooden aqueduct or launder, an overhead construction of heavy timbers, 10 feet wide and 40 yards in length, discharging directly into the wheel pits. The woodwork of the launders and the wheels has been replaced, but the ironwork and the machinery are original. The two largest wheels were made in Tavistock and it is believed that these, as well as the power shears and the trip and drop hammers were originally in use at Tavistock Iron Works. The smaller fan wheel was probably acquired from the former corn mill.

Besides making all the wooden handles it required for its tools, the Foundry also acted as the local blacksmith's shop for the village, and as the wheelwright's shop. Many of the tools were of traditional local patterns, made to suit specialised requirements. The productivity of the men who worked here was formidable. Five men made 400 completely finished swan-neck hoes in a day. The inclusion of a Museum of Rural Industries within the Finch premises has made it possible to pay a proper tribute to the remarkable skill and stamina of the people employed in these small country enterprises.

The Richard Jefferies Museum. *Borough of Thamesdown. Coate Farmhouse, Coate, Swindon, Wiltshire. On the south-eastern outskirts of the town, near the reservoir, Coate Water, just off the A345 to Marlborough. Open W., Sa., Su. 2–5.*

Despite its name, this Museum commemorates, in fact, two local writers, Richard Jefferies and Alfred Williams, the 'Hammerman Poet'. The house came into the possession of the Jefferies family in 1800 and Richard Jefferies, one of our best-known and best-loved writers on nature and the countryside, was born here in 1848. It was bought by Swindon Corporation, now transformed into the Borough of Thamesdown, in 1926 and, much later, restored and opened by the Borough as a museum. The Richard Jefferies exhibits are upstairs, and those relating to Alfred Williams on the ground floor.

Jefferies lived here until he was 26 and afterwards drew on his memories of Coate and the surrounding countryside for the main substance of his books. During his last few years – he was only 39 when he died – he wrote a remarkable amount, despite his poor health, in an attempt to set down a record of rural society which was already disintegrating and of a natural environment he hoped would never change. The immediate surroundings of the old farmhouse are now very different from what they were in Jefferies' day – Swindon has crawled out to its front gate – but the countryside towards the downs is remarkably unchanged.

The little museum dedicated to Jefferies contains early editions of his works, some of his manuscripts and letters, photographs, including a daguerrotype of his mother, and a number of personal possessions. One of the two attic rooms was used by the young Richard Jefferies as a study bedroom. It contains his writing table, which his widow took with her to Perranporth after his death, and the oak chest in which he kept his papers. Before it was acquired by the Museum, the contents of the chest were sold. Among them was the manuscript, in exercise books, of his first novel, a schoolboy adventure story, *Benn Tubb's Adventures*, written when he was 17. It is

The Richard Jefferies Museum, Swindon, Wiltshire.

now, for some reason, at the Fitzwilliam Museum, Cambridge.

Alfred Williams who, so to speak, shares the house with Jefferies, certainly deserves his museum – he is an underrated Victorian writer, the value of whose comments on the life of his times is being increasingly recognised – but somehow Coate Farm hardly seems the place for him, since he had no personal associations with it. Here, he is somewhat in the position of an outsider at a family party, which is never an easy part to play. He was only ten when Jefferies died – he lived on

Bedroom. The Richard Jefferies Museum, Swindon.

until 1930 – and, although his love of the countryside around what was then the railway town of Swindon probably equalled that of Jefferies, he saw life in the district with a double vision, the tyranny and slavery of the railway workshops, where he was forced to earn a living, and the infinitely preferable values of the old agricultural society which, like Jefferies, he saw coming to pieces before his eyes.

Perhaps it was, after all, no bad thing to put both of them together under the same roof and to leave the visitor, suitably prepared by his approach through modern Swindon, to draw his own conclusions.

Somerset County Museum. *Somerset County Council. Taunton Castle, Taunton, Somerset. Open April 1–September 30, M.–Sa. 10–5. October 1– March 31. Tu.–Sa. 10–5.*

Until 1974 Somerset was a real county, but in that disastrous year it was chopped in half as a result of the reorganisation of local government areas. Everything north of Mendip was transferred to the new authority of Avon, which meant that it became an appendage of Bristol, and what remained to the south continued to be Somerset. This left the County Museum at Taunton in a difficult position. Which county, the old or the new, was it supposed to represent? Was it in duty bound to hand over to Bristol or Bath or Weston-super-Mare everything in its collections which related to the northern part of the old county? Or should it discreetly forget about the Local Government Reorganisation Act and hold on to

Somerset County Museum, Taunton.

Right:
Bronze plaque, probably 1st Century AD, from South Cadbury Hill Fort. Somerset County Museum, Taunton.

what was already in its possession? Very sensibly, it chose the second course, so that what is now on show and in store at Taunton represents the history and culture of the old, traditional county, and nobody seems greatly bothered at the decision.

It would have been ungrateful, as well as foolish, to have proceeded in any other way. The Museum had been established in the much modified 12th century Taunton Castle since 1876. Until 1958, when the maintenance of the buildings eventually became too great a burden, it had been in the charge of the Somersetshire Archaeological and Natural History Society, which had been founded in 1849 and which used the Castle as its base of operations. Somerset County Council then took over responsibility for both the Castle and the collections and radical reorganisation of the displays has been carried out during the past ten years.

Now, as in 1958, the main strengths of the Museum are in archaeology, geology and the decorative arts. The archaeological material includes a prehistoric dugout canoe from the peat bog at Shapwick, the notable collections from Meare Lake Village, near Glastonbury, and the superb mosaic pavement from the Roman villa at Low Ham, depicting the story of Dido and Aeneas, but these are only the outstanding items of a very comprehensive and well-displayed range of items which illustrate the culture and settlement of Somerset from Neolithic times onwards. For the modern period, the sections of the Museum most likely to catch the attention of visitors are those devoted to Judge Jefferies and the Monmouth Rebellion, which showed our ancestors at their most vindictive and beastly, and to Ilchester Jail, which was certainly not an agreeable place. The example of leather made from the skin of a prisoner executed there suggests Belsen rather than Somerset. Witches and super-stitions also have their place in the Museum, with exhibits ranging from quaintness to nastiness. Half-way between the two are the ash-trees, split as saplings, through which a child with a hernia could be pulled or pushed, in order to effect a cure.

After such examples of folk culture, the applied arts bring a welcome breath of civilisation – a small but choice collection of Taunton silver, women's costumes and dress accessories from the eighteenth century onwards, and, civilised and beautiful although not, alas, Somerset, a splendid collection of Chinese ceramics, which is just one of these things that county societies and museums used to acquire as a matter of course in the days of wealth, privilege, imperialism and next to no income tax or death duties.

Tiverton Museum. *Tiverton Museum Society. St. Andrew Street, Tiverton, Devon. Open M.–Sa. 10.30–1. 2–4.30.*

Started by volunteer enthusiasts in 1960 in two borrowed rooms, Tiverton Museum is now one of the largest local museums in the West of England. Its present main building is itself a museum piece, the National Schools, built in 1841, but extensions have been required to accommodate the rapidly growing collections.

The theme of the Museum is the history of Tiverton and the surrounding area and this has been interpreted in the widest possible way, with very rich collections ranging from the Devon Regiments to cider-making and from musical instru-ments to local charities. Tiverton means, among many other things, Blundell's School, and this has its appropriate section in the Museum, including relics of R.D. Blackmore and *Lorna Doone*. Boys from the school have, incidentally, spent many hours helping to restore items now displayed in the Museum. The Crime and Punishment exhibit, a natural sequel to Education, includes the stocks from Cullompton and Witteridge, a fine range of truncheons and handcuffs, a grim list of executions and a broadsheet on John Lee, 'the man they couldn't hang'.

The Victoriana are deliciously and somewhat wickedly displayed – old boots superstitiously buried in a cob wall, equipment for making pillow-lace, senti-mental Valentines, a glass pistol which contained sweets, and a cord and clip to hold a long skirt clear of the ground, at a height discreetly chosen to avoid display-ing the ankle. One of the attractive fea-tures of the Museum is that it does not take the Victorian period too seriously.

There is a good Railway Gallery, exhi-bits dealing with the history of the town's

Tiverton Museum, Devon.

The Waggon Gallery. Tiverton Museum.

water supply, disastrous fires, road transport, pharmacy and medicine, royal visits, religion, and local life during two World Wars. The Victorian Laundry has all the appropriate equipment and so does the Village Smithy, brought, complete with tools, from the village of Silverton. There is a purpose-built Waggon Gallery for horse-drawn vehicles, and an Industrial Gallery, which emphasises the importance of Tiverton as an old-established manufacturing centre.

The strongest feature of this excellent museum is, however, undoubtedly its Agricultural Hall, which is almost a mini-museum in itself. It is full of splendid exhibits not often found elsewhere – the salmon-poacher's brazier for luring salmon at night, the so-called Humane Man-Trap, which merely broke the trespasser's leg, instead of tearing it to pieces, the sheep-coupler, a simple device linking two sheep together, so that they could not jump through a gap unless they synchronised their efforts with split-second timing.

The style of presentation is well conveyed by this announcement relating to the Museum's barrel-piano. 'Other duties permitting, an attendant will sometimes play by request, this legacy of the pre-radio era, at visitors' own risk of discord, as it is not invariably at concert pitch.'

Weymouth Museum of Local History. *Weymouth and Portland Museums Service. Westham Road, Weymouth, Dorset. Open April 1–September 30, M., W., Th., F. 10–8; Tu., Sa. 10–5. October 1–March 31, Tu.–Sa. 10–1, 2–5.*

Until the early 1970s there was no museum at all in Weymouth, a strange oversight in a town with such an interesting history. A beginning was made in 1971, with a temporary exhibition to celebrate the four hundredth anniversary of the union of Weymouth and Melcombe Regis. In the following year, the temporary exhibition was promoted to a museum, telling the story of what is now the Borough of Weymouth and Portland.

There are many prehistoric and Roman items from local excavations. They include the skeleton of a young Romano-British woman, found at Radipole in 1978, and the Roman pavement uncovered in Newberry Terrace, Weymouth, in 1902. The Saxon and medieval material is concerned mainly with churches and monasteries, but from Tudor times onwards the range of exhibits is considerably more varied. It includes a treasure chest which formed part of the baggage of

The Armada Chest, reputed to have been brought ashore from the 'San Salvador', July 1588. Weymouth Museum.

Philip and Joan of Castile when they were driven ashore at Weymouth by a storm in 1506. It was, for some reason, left behind in the town; another treasure chest brought ashore from the captured Armada galleon, *San Salvador*, which had been brought into Weymouth Bay as a prize; and a chair once belonging to Weymouth Priory, which was supposed to have the magical power of granting direct and speedy passage to Heaven to anyone who happened to die while sitting in it. Owing to the great age and fragile nature of the chair, the Museum is unfortunately not able to grant this facility to its visitors.

There are exhibits related to the part played by Weymouth in the Civil War and the Monmouth Rebellion. Executing twelve of the convicted rebels cost the town £15 14s. 3d., and there is a detailed list of what became of their heads and quarters. Weymouth really came into its own, however, as a result of the visits of George III between 1789 and 1805. Georgian Weymouth was generously recorded in prints and paintings and the Museum shows a fine selection of them, including a number of cartoons lampooning the Royal Family on holiday. There is also, as one of the greatest prizes in the

collections, the actual bathing machine used by the King during his first visit in 1789.

Although Royal patronage passed to Brighton after the death of George III, Weymouth continued to grow in popularity as a seaside resort in Victorian times and it had a regular service of mailships to the Channel Islands. Both of these aspects of the town's history are reflected in the displays at the Museum and so, too, is the once profitable local industry of smuggling. In 1832 Lieutenant Knight, R.N., of the Preventive Service, was attacked by a local group of smugglers and thrown over the cliff. He died from his injuries, and his memorial stone was given to the Museum when the old town graveyard at Bury Street was closed in 1974.

The exhibits dealing with the later Victorian period and with the 20th century are mostly of a more peaceful and domestic nature, although Weymouth's close links with a Navy, both in peacetime and during two World Wars are well documented, which is as it should be, since without the Navy the local economy would have been in some trouble, especially in the winter months.

Wookey Hole Mill. *Wookey Hole Caves Ltd. Wookey Hole, Wells, Somerset. Open April 1–September 30, daily 10–7. October 1–March 31, daily 10–5.30.*

Wookey Hole, since 1973 an important and much-visited subsidiary of Madame Tussaud's, is really two museums in one, the caves and the paper-mills, and the paper-mills in turn are four separate museums under the same roof – paper-making, fairground equipment, Madame Tussaud's mould store, and prehistoric and Romano-Celtic archaeology. There is evidence of human occupation in the caves between 250 BC and 392 AD, and a mass of human bones broken for the

cooking pot showed that some at least of the people who lived there were not averse to cannibalism, although other finds prove the inhabitants to have practised industry at a fairly advanced level. Spindle whorls, weaving combs, imported Samian ware, and molten metal tipped from a crucible show the cave-dwellers in a different light.

The second part of the Museum tells the story of paper-making at the Mill and demonstrates the processes involved.

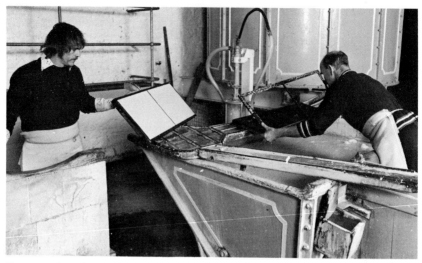

Paper-making by hand at Wookey Hole Mill.

High-quality paper was made at Wookey Hole early in the 17th century. Between 1800 and 1850 many Somerset mills closed and the four vats at Wookey Hole were reduced to two. At that point the Hodgkinson family bought the property. They were London wholesale stationers and they built nearly everything one can see there today. They installed steam power – the mill had used only water power until they arrived – and they controlled production until 1961 when they sold out to the Inveresk Paper Company. During their time the mill's demand for labour quadrupled the population of the village. Wookey Hole Mill reached the peak of its fame and prosperity during the first decade of the present century, when there were fourteen vats in operation. The new lofts, opened in 1900 when Victorian patriotism was also booming, were named Kimberley, Ladysmith and Pretoria. When paper-making came to an end here in 1972, both the buildings and the machinery were in a rundown condition and a great deal of restoration was needed before the mill could be re-opened as a museum.

The remaining sections of the Museum, although interesting in themselves, have no connection with Wookey Hole or with life in the area at any period. They are here simply because they are here and they could just as suitably be in Brighton or Blackpool. Lady Bangor's celebrated collection of fairground equipment arrived in 1973 and at about the same time Madame Tussaud's decided that the old drying lofts of the paper mill would be ideal for storing the moulds and reference duplicates of the heads of celebrities on display in Baker Street, together with the huge library of leg and torso negatives.

Madame Tussaud's is not only the new owner of Wookey Mill: it is the new local industry. If the old buildings had not received this transfusion of money they might well have been demolished by now. Roundabouts, fairground organs and moulds for the waxworks are the subsidy which allows us to continue to watch paper being made in the traditional way by hand at Wookey. No harm is done by being grateful.

The Channel Islands

Alderney Society Museum. *The Old School, Alderney, Channel Islands. 'There are very few mornings in the year when it is not open from 10 a.m. to 12.30, and also, when possible, on wet afternoons.'*

This is one of the most genuinely democratic museums in the British Isles, started and run entirely by volunteers. When it began in 1966, its quarters were a group of basement rooms of the Island Hall, but in 1972 the opportunity arose, and was seized, to move into an agreeable old building dating from 1790, which spent much of its earlier life as the Island's school.

Alderney is only 3½ miles long and 1½ miles across but, as generations of pirates, exiles and seafaring men have discovered, it is conveniently close to the French coast and, as a result, it has a history which is much more interesting than its size might suggest, a fact which has been greatly to the advantage of the Alderney Society and its Museum. The Island has, in fact, been continuously inhabited since Neolithic times and what the visitor to the Museum is shown is the visible record of 2,560 years of local life.

The survey starts, properly enough, at the beginning, with a large collection of Iron Age 'A' pottery and tools found during the course of archaeological excavations on Alderney. Moving about over the two and a half millenia since then, we are shown a good collection of craft and trade tools, the military badges and other mementoes of the regiments stationed here from the 18th century onwards, the machinery from the original Alderney lighthouse and a number of medals, weapons, tools and general relics from the German occupation, which lasted five long years, from 1940 to 1945. A particularly interesting and moving section deals with the great difficulties faced by the people of Alderney when they returned home to a derelict Island after the war.

Although it was not originally planned

Alderney Society Museum, Channel Islands.

in this way, the Museum has gradually taken on the role of a Tourist Office. Most visitors come to the Museum for information of all kinds. It is the centre of Alderney's cultural life and of a good deal of its social life, too.

Folk Museum, Saumarez Park. *National Trust of Guernsey. Saumarez Park, Câtel, Guernsey, Channel Islands. Open mid-March–October 31, daily 10–12.30, 2–6.*

The Folk Museum was started in 1968, in co-operation with the Société Guernesiaise, with a collection of farm implements made by the late Advocate Langlois and added to by the Société over the years. The Museum is housed in the old stables of Saumarez Park and is designed to show the way of life of the rural community of Guernsey in the 19th century.

The Museum is not a large one, but a great deal is made of a relatively small space. Much use is made of reconstructed room-settings – the Kitchen (la Tchuisaene), the largest room in the house, where the family lived, worked and entertained, the Bedroom, with the farmer's wife in a half-tester bed with her new baby; the Wash-House, with a wash day in progress; the Dairy, showing preparation for market, with butter being made, a boy bringing water from the pump, curds and eggs ready.

The Costume Room displays costumes, hats, gloves, and shoes, samplers, lace and needlework; the Cart Room has a collection of vehicles, including a horse bus and a long cart with a double ox-yoke; the centrepiece of the Plough Room, upstairs, is a Guernsey Great Plough, set out for a mixed team of an ox and a horse.

The Toolroom, also upstairs, shows

Above: Part of the Costume Collection, Guernsey Folk Museum.

granite and other Guernsey building materials, with examples and site-photographs of thatch, slate and plaster. A quarryman is splitting stone and, on the end wall, there is an exhibit of agricultural hand tools, with a number of highly specialised items among them – a seaweed fork (fourque à vraic), a dock digger (bêquot à doques), and a parsnip digger (fourque à posnais) are only three. The Cider Barn, next to the Tool Room, contains the crusher, which is driven by a horse-gear and fed with apples from the loft above. There is a press, dated 1734, with a splendid wooden screw. On one of the walls is a 1787 map, showing where the cider apple orchards used to be.

'We present Island life in 1870,' says the National Trust, 'to a host of visitors from the U.K.', and no doubt the Museum does have an important function as a tourist attraction. But it is a dignified and sensible attraction and one which helps Guernsey people as well as mainlanders from both sides of the Channel to realise and maybe mourn the individuality that has been lost.

Guernsey Museum and Art Gallery. *Ancient Monuments Committee. Candie Gardens, St. Peter Port, Guernsey, Channel Islands. Open daily 10.30–5.30.*

Before 1978, when this new museum opened, Guernsey was in the somewhat strange situation of having a fort museum, a maritime museum, and a tomato museum, but no museum telling the story of the Island as a whole. The States of Guernsey therefore decided to set up such a museum, in new buildings designed specially for the purpose. They wisely made up their minds to do the job properly, with a first-class architect, a first-class designer and a first-class scriptwriter. They also gave the new museum a superb site high up in the Candie Gardens, with fine views over the sea, the town and the neighbouring islands, and by appointing a Curator before planning began, they made sure that the project would go forward as a team effort from the beginning. Few museums can ever have started in more favourable circumstances and it is hardly surprising that this one received the prestigious Museum of the Year Award in 1979.

The building is ingenious. Formed of a cluster of interlocking octagons, it echoes the shape of the Victorian bandstand which was already on the site and which, suitably restored and modified, has been transformed into the Museum tea-room and skilfully incorporated into the new complex. Light and cheerful, the architecture fits excellently into the elegance and holiday atmosphere of St. Peter Port and adds further charm to the garden setting.

Visitors are encouraged to begin their tour in the audio-visual theatre, where they are given a very comfortable sound and vision introduction to the island and the museum. This area leads directly into the art gallery and main display sections. In the middle of the last century Guernsey had two artists, Paul Jacob Naftel and Peter Le Lievre, who spent much of their time painting scenes, mostly watercolours, of their native island. Their paintings present Guernsey in a charming and comprehensive way, illustrating how it was before tourists and tomatoes became Guernsey's principal sources of income. Other major collections now housed here and very attractively displayed are the bequests of Frederick Corbin Lukis,

Guernsey Museum and Art Gallery.

Jersey's pioneer archaeologist and founder of the island's first museum; and Wilfred Carey's collection of pictures, prints and ceramics. Great care has been taken in planning and arranging the museum to avoid anything of an exotic nature. The art gallery, like the rest of the museum, exists primarily to tell visitors about Guernsey, and what is on exhibition there blends easily and naturally with the other displays.

The story of Guernsey, as told in the Museum, begins very properly with the rocks of which it is formed – the granites. Their durable nature was able to withstand the battering of the sea after the ice retreated north and thus the Channel

Islands were formed nine thousand years ago. The characteristic rock is evident throughout the Island in the simple houses and solid farm buildings. The pattern of history in the Channel Islands, agreeably illustrated by the displays in the new Museum, was very different from that of Southern Britain or of the neighbouring parts of France. After an interesting and continuous period of Stone Age, Bronze Age and Iron Age settlement, Guernsey, like the rest of the Islands, disappeared from the record after the Roman conquests of Gaul and Britain cut the old trade routes across and along the Channel. The Roman and Saxon periods, which have provided such an important part of the stock-in-trade of mainland museums, are unrepresented in

76

76 THE GUERNSEY TOMATO CENTRE

Guernsey, where the Dark Ages came to an end when the Normans added the island to their territory in 933, more than a century before they ventured across the Channel to England. From then onwards, the harbours and fortifications of Guernsey, strategically placed between England and France, were the basis of its importance and prosperity. Neither fully English nor fully French, the culture of Guernsey has a reality and a charm of its own, with a quieter atmosphere and less obvious commercial zest than Jersey and with a strong community spirit which has somehow allowed the essence of the old traditions to be maintained against all comers.

The Museum reflects all this in a particularly skilful and appealing way. Conceived in the first instance mainly for the benefit of the islanders themselves, to show them what their roots were and to encourage their morale and self-respect, it has an equal interest for visitors from outside. No-one can leave the Museum without feeling that Guernsey is different and that, in an age of standardisation and uniformity, is a very great tribute.

The Guernsey Tomato Centre. *Guernsey Tomato Centre Ltd. King's Mills, Guernsey, Channel Islands. Open Easter–September 30, daily 10–5.*

Tomato growing is Guernsey's most important industry and that the Island should have a tomato museum is entirely fit and proper. It is, however, a very recent development – the opening date was April 1977 – and it has been planned to show the enormous changes which have taken place since the first commercial crop was grown less than a century ago, in the 1880s.

The museum, or to give it its correct name, the Guernsey Tomato Centre, con-

The Guernsey Tomato Centre, Guernsey.

sists of a group of glasshouses, built at various dates between the 1890s and the 1970s. Four of these are growing crops – mainly tomatoes, but with some grapes, carnations and friesias – to illustrate the history of the glasshouse industry in Guernsey and the others contain a cinema; a museum which has remarkably comprehensive collections of old tomato-growing equipment; a most agreeable café, in which one can take refreshments in the leafy, flowery surroundings of a conservatory; and an ingenious display of the main vegetables grown in Guernsey, with a mural painting of them along one wall and the vegetables themselves flourishing in a broad bed running in front of the painting. A garden-centre type of shop, in which one can buy tomato-growing kits of various sizes and degrees of complexity, as well, of course, as tomatoes grown on the spot, completes the arrangement.

This is a living, working museum of an unfamiliar kind and one which will surely be initated for other types of crops. One already hears talk, for example, of a Museum of Sweet Corn on the Isle of Wight. It presents, in practical, imaginative ways which make the information stay in the memory, the kind of facts which are likely to come as a surprise to most people – that the weight of tomatoes produced per plant in Guernsey has gone up from 10 pounds to 30 pounds during the past 15 years; that the glasshouse pioneers originally grew tomatoes only as an extra, underneath the principal crop, grapes; that until two-thirds of the way through last century most people· considered raw tomatoes highly poisonous, so that the plants were grown chiefly for ornamental purposes.

We should not, of course, overlook one of the Tomato Centre's most enterprising innovations, Aztecato, a white wine made entirely from tomatoes and tasting not unlike a good quality non-resinated Greek wine. The name, which commemorates the South American origins of the tomato, is a welcome addition both to the oenophile's vocabulary and to his range of experience. The 1976 vintage, available in 1979, was almost as strong as a non-fortified wine can be.

The Jersey Museum. *Société Jersiaise. 9 Pier Road, St. Helier, and La Hougue Bie, Grouville, Jersey, Channel Islands. At Pier Road, open February–December, M.–Sa. 10–5. At La Hougue Bie, open late March–October 31, Tu.–Su. 10–5.*

The Jersey Museum is owned and managed by the Société Jersiaise, a voluntary organisation founded in 1873 to study and preserve the antiquities and natural history of the Island. Its headquarters in Pier Road was built c.1815 as a merchant's house. Like the prehistoric tomb at La Hougue Bie, it is made of granite, the traditional Jersey building material.

The history and culture of Jersey have been influenced very much by its location, which has made it a strange mixture of French and English. Its economic activity – fishing, farming, privateering, trading and shipbuilding – has reflected this. Today its main industries are banking and foreign tax evasion, tourism and agriculture/horticulture, in that order. A combination of these and other factors has helped to develop the individuality of Jersey's customs, institutions, natural history and economy. The Museum displays illustrate many aspects of this uniqueness.

The Jersey Museum, Channel Islands.

As with many islands, Jersey's flora and fauna include sub-species which have developed in isolation from other breeding colonies. Equally, some wild creatures, such as the hare and the fox, are not found in Jersey. The Natural History collections illustrate these peculiarities and the Marine Biology Room, refreshingly arranged in the now exotic pre-1914 style, has a fine collection of ormers, spider crabs, conger eels and other inhabitants of the seas around the Channel Island coasts.

Elsewhere in the Museum, there are exhibits devoted to the Jersey-born actress and friend of Royalty, Lillie Langtry, to the shipping magnate and racing yacht owner, T.B. Davis, to postal history and to the German occupation.

There are mementoes of the old prison in St. Helier, including the treadmill, manacles and cell doors, two Victorian period rooms – a parlour and a bedroom – the kitchen and bedroom of a typical farmhouse, and a Shiproom, which illustrates Jersey's maritime history and shipbuilding. The fittings of a recently modernised St. Helier chemist's shop have been used in the Museum's reconstruction of a Victorian pharmacy.

The Barreau Art Gallery contains pictures by famous Jersey artists of the past, including Millais, as well as works by contemporary local painters and by non-Jersey artists who painted local scenes.

At La Hougue Bie, 3 miles from St. Helier, the Society's branch museum has as its central feature a massive Neolithic tomb, dating from c.3000 BC. The tomb is within a 40-foot high mound, which is crowned by two medieval chapels. Also inside the mound, but causing no damage to the tomb, the Germans who occupied the Island between 1940 and 1945 constructed an elaborate concrete dugout. The Jersey Society has prudently and economically converted this into a Museum of the Occupation. At the La Hougue Bie site, which comprises several acres of pleasant countryside, are also the Museum's collections relating to archaeology, geology, agriculture and rural crafts. The agricultural section is concerned particularly with Jersey farming as it used to be in Victorian and Edwardian times, and among the exhibits likely to be unfamiliar to visitors from the French and English mainlands are an example of the special Jersey haycart, the Hèrnais à Éclon, and the six-horse plough, the Grand' Tchéthue. A restored guard's van of the Jersey Eastern Railway contains an exhibition designed to serve as a reminder of the two railway companies, both now long deceased, which used to operate on the Island.

'The Jersey Lily', Jersey-born actress Lillie Langtry. The Jersey Museum, Channel Islands.

The East

The Manor House. *West Street, Alford, Lincolnshire. Alford and District Civic Trust. Open May 30–September 10, M., Tu., W., F. 10.30–12.30 and 2–4. Closed remainder of year.*

'This Museum,' says the Curator, 'is one of the few in this part of the country which illustrates the life of ordinary people in ordinary houses, as opposed to stately homes.' This is probably true, but it does depend to some extent, of course, on what one means by 'ordinary people' and 'ordinary houses'. The Manor House is in fact, by modern standards, quite a large house, occupied in its time by lawyers and landowners. With its stables, walled garden, nine bedrooms and splendid Tudor hall, it was never exactly a cottage. But it is a very nice house and it makes a very nice museum.

Much of the present building is 18th or 19th century, but the oldest parts date back to about 1540. Since it acquired the property by gift in 1967, the Civic Trust has carried out extensive restoration work, particular attention being paid to opening up the original Tudor timber frame which was bricked over in about 1700. As it is now arranged, the Manor House cleverly combines museum-type displays and the architectural features and decorations of the house itself to illustrate change and development in the district over a period of several centuries. The Hall contains accounts of Alford in the Middle Ages and of the building of the Manor House; the dining room and 19th century kitchen have the appropriate Victoriana; the Tudor kitchen contains, not a Tudor, but a Victorian street scene, with a sweet shop, chemist's shop, cobbler's shop, veterinary surgery, and photographer's shop; the attics, where the servants huddled at night time, also have the nursery, the schoolroom and, as a new museum area, an archaeology display which illustrates settlement in the area from Neolithic to Roman times.

Chemist's Shop c. 1900. The Manor House Folk Museum, Alford, Lincolnshire.

The Wash House provides suitable accommodation for a fine variety of mangles and other ancient wash-day equipment and the Stables and Outhouses for Agricultural and Transport Gallery exhibits. A nice touch in the Transport Gallery is a Porter's Room, with the platform outside, to illustrate Alford in the railway age, a period of a little over a century, which began in 1848 and lasted until it was brought to a sharp and brutal end by Dr. Beeching's axe.

Opposite, above:
Folk Museum, Saumarez Park, Guernsey, Channel Islands.

Opposite, below:
The Guernsey Tomato Centre, Channel Islands.

Opposite:
The back of Gainsborough's House, Sudbury, Suffolk.

Above:
Tudor fireplace. Cambridge Folk Museum.

Cambridge and County Folk Museum. *Trustees of the Folk Museum. 2–3 Castle Street, Cambridge. Open Tu.–F. 10.30–5; Sa. 10.30–1, 2–5; Su. 2.30–4.30.*

The Museum was started as a private foundation in 1936 and it has succeeded in preserving its independence ever since. The Museum building, which dates from the 16th century, was once the White Horse Inn. Its ten rooms contain exhibits gathered from the City and County of Cambridge and the Isle of Ely, illustrating the daily life and work of the people of this area from medieval times until the beginning of the present century. Except in the rooms devoted to the City and University, Rural Life and Fens and Folklore, the Museum makes no clear distinction between town objects and country objects. The field is the county as a whole.

So, for example, in the Trades and Occupations section we find the tools and implements of the thatcher, brickmaker, basketmaker and straw plaiter side by side with those of the bootmaker, chemist, barber, tobacconist and chimney sweep. There is the tray, head-pall and bell of the Cambridge muffin-man for good measure and in the Kitchen department there are sugar-loaf cutters, hand-operated vacuum cleaner, mice, beetle and bed-bug traps and goffering equipment.

But it is in Rooms 8 and 9, the country rooms, where the visitor is most likely to feel that he really is in contact with a vanished age, the age of hand tools, self sufficiency and rural ingenuity. Here we can see the set of box bells which, fixed to the hames on a horse's collar, gave warning of the approach of a waggon on a narrow country lane; the sparrow pot, fixed under the eaves of a house to attract sparrows to nest in it, rather than in the thatch of the roof; the dulcimer, made at Haslingfield in 1886 and played at rural feasts and fairs; a breast plough, which a man pushed with his chest to pare turf from land that was to be reclaimed; the basket in which the famous Cambridge yard butter was carried, the boards used for shaping the yard-long rolls by hand and the yardstick for measuring them.

The Fens and Folklore room, however, has the greatest concentration of rarities and oddities. There are overshoes fitted to the back feet of horses to stop them sinking into the Fenland mud; a loaf baked on Good Friday, which was supposed never to go mouldy, to bring good luck if kept in the house and to be a cure for digestive troubles if it was grated into a warm drink; the horse's jawbone built into the wall of a 17th century house to protect the occupants against witchcraft.

From such strange things, it is reassuring to be able to inspect the three-wheeled roller skates designed by A.E. Tebbitt, British Amateur Ice-Skating Champion in 1895, 1900 and 1902. He used them on the roads near his farm at Waterbeach, to keep himself in practice for skating on ice.

Easton Farm Park. *Easton Farm Park (Suffolk) Ltd. Easton, Woodbridge, Suffolk. Take the B1116 off the A12 half a mile north of Wickham Market and follow signs to Easton. Open mid-April–end of first week in October, 10.30–6.*

Easton Farm Park was opened to the public in 1974. It was established by James Kerr, who had a notable collection of early farm machinery. The 35 acres which now form the park were previously part of the Kerr family's farming business.

The red brick farm buildings were built by the Duke of Hamilton in the 1870s as a model dairy farm on his Easton estate. There was no farmhouse; it was essentially a working unit. The buildings included the very latest in dairies, with Victorian Gothic windows and doors, stained glass, a central fountain, and William Morris-style decorations, the estate laundry and two farm cottages, one for the farm foreman and the other for the laundrymaids and dairymaids. A herd of Red Polls was milked in the two small cowsheds and one can still see the stables for the working horses, Suffolk Punches.

Visitors to the Museum are able to compare the 1870 buildings with a large modern dairy unit completed in 1976. It has been designed to incorporate viewing

1886 Ransomes, Sims and Jefferies steam-run seed huller. Easton Farm Park, Suffolk.

facilities – there is an overhead catwalk for this purpose – and it allows one man to milk 130 cows a day. In 1870 the Head Dairymaid and her two assistants milked 23 cows.

The Farm Museum has a number of traditional breeds of cattle, horses, and sheep on show, including some which are on the list of the Rare Breeds Survival Trust, formed in 1973 to preserve breeds of domestic livestock which are in danger of extinction. There is also a large collection of farm machinery, presented to illustrate the steady mechanisation of agriculture since the late nineteenth century. East Anglia, and Suffolk in particular – one of the most prosperous agricultural areas in the country – was where much of this development took place. The Museum has good representative collections of the machines made by these firms, and arranges demonstrations of some of them. The steam threshing days are especially popular.

A wide range of country bygones is distributed throughout the farm build-

Victorian Dairy, Easton Farm Park, Suffolk.

Highland cattle at Easton Farm Park, Suffolk.

ings. The exhibition in the Victorian Dairy is more or less permanent, with a fairly complete collection of the equipment which would have been used there in Victorian times, but the other displays are changed frequently, to avoid the wasteful situation, found in so many museums, of having perhaps one tenth of the collection on show and nine-tenths always in store doing nothing. This is, in fact, an unusually and refreshingly economical museum.

Nothing is wasted. A well-explained Nature Trail guides visitors round the four natural habitats on the Model Farm, the ditches and streams, the damp woodland, the grassland and the river, and draws attention to all the plants and wild creatures that are likely to be found there at different seasons of the year, from Red Admiral butterflies to watercress and from goldfinches to stinging nettles.

Maritime Museum for East Anglia. *Norfolk Museums Service. Marine Parade, Great Yarmouth, Norfolk. Opposite the Bathing Pool. Open June 1–September 30, daily 10–1, 2–8. October 1–May 31, M.–F. 10–1, 2–5.30*

Yarmouth has five museums, which combine to present a comprehensive picture of the history of the town. Much of its prosperity in the past was based on fishing, and particularly on the great shoals of herring which appeared offshore in the autumn. The herring has now almost vanished from the North Sea, but the *Lydia Eva*, the last steam drifter built

Opposite:
Maritime Museum for East Anglia, Great Yarmouth, Norfolk.

Below:
Model of the Yarmouth herring lugger Edward *c. 1850. Maritime Museum, Great Yarmouth.*

to fish from Yarmouth, was bought in 1969 by the newly established Maritime Trust and since 1973 she has been moored at South Quay, near the Town Hall, and administered by the Norfolk Museums Service as a floating museum on behalf of the Trust.

She is, so to speak, Part One of Yarmouth's Maritime Museum. Part Two is in a building opened in 1861 as a club for sailors and a home for shipwrecked mariners. Over the years, visiting seamen presented the club with curios acquired in foreign parts, and eventually these became sufficiently numerous to be formed into a small museum, which was open to the public. By the 1960s the building had become redundant and it was transferred, together with its museum, to the Corporation of the town. Expanded and properly displayed, the collection then became the present Maritime Museum.

In its new form, the Museum illustrates the many ways in which the sea has affected the life-style of people in East Anglia and provided so many of them with a livelihood. The Museum collections cover herring fishing gear, ship models – there is an especially fine one of a sailing lugger hauling in her nets, made in about 1850 – boat-building tools, life-saving apparatus, and navigation instruments. The early life-saving devices are particularly interesting. They include those invented by a Norfolk man, Captain George Manby (1765-1854) – a mortar apparatus for firing a line on to a ship wrecked near the shore, a lifeboat with buoyancy chambers, and the breeches buoy. Manby used working models to illustrate the lectures in which he tried to interest people in life-saving, and in 1838 he presented his models and drawings to Norwich Museum.

The Museum is enlivened by an interesting display of jumping jacks, the toys and ornaments made by sailors and lightship crews in their spare time. These include Aunt Sally dolls, engraved whale teeth, and ships in bottles. In recent years, good examples of these, such as the Museum possesses, have become much sought after by collectors.

The Maritime Museum also owns the lateen-rigged *Maria*, built in 1827. She was an early Broads racing yacht and one of the best known and most successful of her type.

Norfolk Rural Life Museum. *Norfolk Museums Service. Beech House, Gressenhall, Dereham, Norfolk. 2 miles north-west of East Dereham on the B1146. Open summer months, Tu.–Sa. 10–5; Su. 2–5.30. Times may vary: check with Norfolk Museums Service (0603-22233).*

The Museum, opened in 1976, is installed in one of Britain's largest and architecturally most distinguished workhouses, a fine brick structure of 1777, with a chapel to match.

Norfolk is primarily a rural county and for generations it has led the way in agriculture. Its Rural Life Museum tells the story of its farming over the last 200 years, its country crafts and industries and the life of its country people. Special attention is paid to the famous Norfolk four-course rotation – winter corn, spring corn, roots and clover – which revolutionised agricultural practice in Britain at the end of the 18th century. Innovations in farming, as in everything else, are made and applied by people, and the Museum pays full attention to the men who brought about the changes – the land-

Norfolk Rural Life Museum, Gressenhall, Norfolk.

Wheelwright's Shop. Norfolk Rural Life Museum, Gressenhall.

owners, like Coke and Townshend, who had the money, the originality of mind and the determination to get the pioneering ideas started, and the skilled men and labourers who had the task of making the new machines and the new methods work. The fact that the Museum is in a former workhouse shows that progress had its human victims; the inmates there were the casualties of the system and the size of the buildings is evidence that there were a lot of them.

The collection of tools and implements is very fine and great pains have been taken to relate them to the jobs for which they were designed. The larger machines and the carts and waggons are displayed in what used to be the inner courtyard of the workhouse, now roofed over as a result of the fund-raising energies of the Friends of the Museum. There is an excellent collection of steam and internal combustion engines, some of which can be seen working at special events. The Museum is, by the way, one of the county's principal meeting places for a wide range of activities connected with the countryside. It is by no means only a Museum.

'Rural Life' is interpreted in a broad sense. The Museum's Craftsmen's Row, houses a number of reconstructions of craft workshops – a saddlery, a basket-maker's shop, a wheelwright's premises, a smithy and a village bakery. Experts can be seen at work in Craftsmen's Row from time to time. Another major feature is Cherry Tree Cottage, a typical village cottage of about 1900, reconstructed and furnished with the help of the Norfolk Women's Institutes. The garden is being cultivated as it would have been at the turn of the century, with many of the old fashioned varieties of fruits and flowers that have since gone out of favour.

The Museum is unusually considerate to the aged, infirm and handicapped. There are no stairs to climb and all the doorways are wide enough for wheel-chairs.

The Farmland Museum. *Privately owned. 50 High Street, Haddenham, Cambridgeshire. Open on the first Sunday of every month, 2–dusk. Parties by appointment only, on any evening April–September.*

No museum in the British Isles can have had more remarkable origins than this one. 50 High Street has a large garden. Until the early 1920s it belonged to the farm next door. It then became neglected and overgrown, but during the 1939-45 War it was ploughed up and used for market gardens. In the Fifties it was put down to grass and then, in 1969, ploughed up once more. This time a sharp-eyed small boy, Craig Delanoy, was on hand. He picked up bits of pottery, fragments of clay pipes and anything else which took his fancy, classified and arranged it all neatly in cardboard boxes and announced that, on payment of a fee, anybody could see his museum collection. The money raised was to 'help children who couldn't see and couldn't walk'.

The Museum prospered, more and more items were given to add to the collections, and the entire garden, in the open and under cover, is now the setting for the exhibits. Hundreds of people come on the open days and the entrance fees still go to children's charities.

The first sector is called The Home. It contains a huge variety of domestic items, ranging from wooden washtubs to sausage-fillers and from a fine assembly of flat-irons to toasting forks. There is a comprehensive dairying exhibit – producing, processing and selling milk has been an important feature of Haddenham farming for many years – but some of the most recent items have been the most difficult to find. A machine for putting the cardboard tops on the old wide-topped bottles was brought in relatively early, but the bottles themselves were another matter. However, several from the two local dairies have recently come to light.

A blacksmith's forge and wheelwright's shop have been constructed from old materials and a large collection of hand tools built up, almost entirely with the help of farmworkers and scrap-iron merchants. Outside, there are more than 60 examples of horse-drawn farm imple-

The Farmland Museum, Haddenham, Cambridgeshire.

Model farm labourer. The Farmland Museum, Haddenham, Cambridgeshire.

ments, including several used for growing sugar-beet, an important local crop.

A fourth building was completed in 1976. It is designed so that visitors in wheelchairs can enter it and go round easily and some of the cases are very low, to allow children to see into them. It provides accommodation for a local history exhibit, a display of women's crafts, and rooms illustrating 'How we used to live'. The first museum building, the garden shed, is now used for Natural History, Geology and Archaeology, specially arranged with children in mind. Among the favourite items here is a bone of a dinosaur, found in the local brick pits.

This has been very much a family and community enterprise, but it has been carried out as professionally as possible and with constant expert advice, especially in the important matter of conservation.

The Lynn Museum. *Norfolk Museums Service. Market Street and 27 King Street, King's Lynn, Norfolk. Open Tu.–Sa. 10–5.*

Above:
The Lynn Museum, King's Lynn, Norfolk.

King's Lynn has a long-established tradition of trading with the Continent, and its maritime and commercial history provides the major basis of the collections in the town's museum, which is housed in two separate buildings, the first a former nonconformist chapel and the second in an 18th century merchant's house. Together, these two museum units offer a survey of the natural history and historical development of King's Lynn and the surrounding area of North and West Norfolk. Broadly speaking, the division is, social history at 27 King Street and everything else at Market Street, but the distinction is not a rigid one and there is, inevitably and desirably, a certain amount of overlap between the two groups of collections.

The natural history section is concerned mainly with illustrating the ecology of this part of Norfolk, but there are one or two exotic specimens of particular local interest, notably the stuffed tiger which once stood in Sandringham House and the golden eagle which, regrettably, was shot at Hunstanton at the turn of the century.

The archaeology display traces the development of human culture in Norfolk from Neolithic times to the Saxon period. The exhibits include an important Bronze Age hoard from Hunstanton and a Viking stirrup from Reffley. An interesting medieval collection is distinguished by a fine range of pottery and by a large number of pilgrim badges, which draw attention to the importance of Norfolk as a pilgrimage centre at this time.

The history of Lynn itself is presented from a number of different angles. Many exhibits show the relationship between the town and the sea and with the farming communities of the area, and among the industrial items are a group illustrating the achievements of a local engineering company which has for a long time been one of the world's foremost specialists in the construction of fairground rides.

The social history museum at King Street is housed in a building which is of considerable charm and architectural interest in its own right. During the first half of the 19th century it was the town house of the Everards, who traded in wine and timber and had a bank on the premises. It was opened as a museum in 1973. There are rooms devoted to toys, costume and accessories, and glass, with two further rooms furnished as a

The Lynn Museum, King's Lynn, Norfolk.

Victorian parlour and kitchen. The collection of kitchen and scullery equipment is exceptionally good. There is also a local history gallery and a brass-rubbing centre, where visitors are welcome to try their hand, in exchange for a small fee. On Saturday mornings, children can practise their skill and work off energy for nothing.

Lowestoft Maritime Museum. *Lowestoft and East Suffolk Maritime Society. Sparrows Nest Park, Lowestoft, Suffolk. At the north end of the town, off the A12, below Lowestoft High Lighthouse. Open May 1–October 31, daily, including public holidays, 10–1, 2–sunset.*

The Museum, opened in 1968, is housed in a flint-built cottage, with a recently completed extension at the back. It specialises in the history of the renowned local fishing fleet, especially during the period when vast quantities of herrings were caught in the North Sea by the combined Scottish and East Anglian fleets. Lowestoft has never been a deep-sea fishing port. Its boats have caught their fish in the North Sea, which made it possible to get the catch to market quickly and consequently fresh. Family firms often engaged in several branches of the trade – owning and operating the boats, processing the fish, retailing and export-

ing it.

The Museum shows the history of the industry in all its branches and with the great changes of scale and technology which have taken place over the hundred years of Lowestoft's development as a fishing port. The displays include original equipment of all kinds, a wide range of old photographs, documents and models. There are also several important special collections and curiosities – a group of 'primitive' paintings of local fishing vessels, a number of paintings by Burwood, a local artist active in the 1870s and 1880s, who specialised in painting the East Anglian fishing fleets, and a fine

Lowestoft Maritime Museum, Suffolk.

series of photographs showing the
development of the Port of Lowestoft
from 1885 onwards. There is also a
remarkable mechanical picture of a fishing smack and small boat, which move up
and down as if at sea when the clockwork
mechanism is wound up.

One sad reminder of the grand old days
is the Prunier Trophy, presented by
Madame Prunier, of fish-restaurant fame,
which was competed for during the
autumn fishing season by drifters belonging to the East Anglian and Scottish
fleets.

The Museum has been staffed and run
from the beginning entirely by members
of the Society, so that visitors can count
on enthusiastic, friendly and well-
informed answers to their queries.

*Models of sailing, steam and motor fish-
ing vessels and associated equipment.
Lowestoft Maritime Museum.*

Saffron Walden Museum. *Saffron Walden Museum Society and Uttlesford District Council. Museum Street, Saffron Walden, Essex. Near Parish Church. Open April1–September 30, M.–Sa. 11–5; Su., Bank Holidays, 2.30–5. October 1–March 31, M.–Sa. 11–4; Su., Bank Holidays, 2.30–5.*

This is one of the oldest museums in Britain. The nucleus of the collections was formed in 1832, by the newly established Natural History Society, and two years later the present museum building was erected, at the expense of Lord Braybrooke of Audley End, as a centre for a number of local societies. In 1879 it was taken over entirely by the Museum. Until 1958, it was controlled by Trustees, but in that year control was handed over to a Museum Society. The system since 1974 has been that the District Council has responsibility for administration, but the Society retains ownership of the buildings and collections, a rare division of function.

The quality and scope of the collections is far greater than one would expect in a

Saffron Walden Museum, Essex.

small county museum. The reason for this is interesting: what exists here at Saffron Walden is to a considerable extent a museum of the tastes of local collectors, who eventually presented their treasures to the Trustees. The fine range of Palaeolithic tools on display, for example, was brought together by amateur archaeologists in the 19th and early 20th centuries from many areas of Britain and from other countries as well, and the same is true of the other archaeological and historical sections and of the natural history galleries as well. There is plenty of Essex and East Anglian material, but it takes its places in the general panorama.

Costume, domestic crafts, dolls and toys, weapons and armour, musical instruments – all these parts of the Museum follow the same pattern. Essex items are

English glass posset c. 1680
Saffron Walden Museum, Essex

The Old Woman who lived in a shoe.
Set of jointed dolls presented to a five year old school
girl as a special prize for needlework in 1860.
Saffron Walden Museum, Essex.

English glass posset c. 1680. Saffron Walden Museum.

A needlework sample 1860. Saffron Walden Museum.

there on merit, not as of right. With the documents, it is different. The Museum has a large collection of documents reflecting various aspects of local history – the agricultural societies, charities, industries, education, religious activities, the railways, elections, the Saffron Walden pageant and many others. This type of material is damaged by continuous exposure to light, but selections are made from time to time for temporary exhibitions.

In going round this most attractively arranged Museum, with its unusually rich collections, one finds one's attention moving all the time from the objects to the donors, which is no bad thing, since in its special way Saffron Walden Museum illustrates the character and interests of at least one part of county society during that period of our history which was

brought to an abrupt end by the First World War. These indefatigable and knowledgeable collectors of Roman pottery, Delftware, medieval weapons and Tahitian skirts had the leisure and the money to satisfy their enthusiasm and the public spirit to give or bequeath them to their local museum. One longs at Saffron Walden for a new kind of guide to bring them out of the shadows.

Church Farm Museum. *Lincolnshire Museums. Church Road South, Skegness, Lincolnshire. Open April 1–October 31, daily 10.30–5.30.*

For many years Church Farm formed part of the estates of the Earls of Scarborough, who were responsible for the development of Skegness as a seaside resort at the end of the 19th century. The purchase of the site by the District Council for housing development coincided with the County Council's acquisition of the large collection of farm implements and machinery which had been brought together by Mr. Bernard Best of Bratoft. The District Council has originally intended to demolish the buildings, but agreed instead to offer them to the County Council as a home for the Best Collection. After extensive restoration work had been carried out, the Museum opened in 1976, as an annexe to the Museum of Lincolnshire Life in Lincoln.

The main part of the farmhouse was built about 1760. During the Victorian period, the thatched roof was replaced by pantiles and the porch, wash-house, scullery and pantry were added. By 1900 the house looked much as it does now and for

Church Farm Museum, Skegness, Lincolnshire.

this reason it was decided to base the furnishing on the period 1900-1910. There were people still alive who remembered the house at that time and their memories helped a great deal in the reconstruction. What visitors see is typical of the home of a small Lincolnshire tenant farmer at the beginning of the century.

The wash-house contains its original copper, the living-room has the cupboard by the side of the fireplace for storing jam and home-made wine and the large larder illustrates the self-sufficiency of country houses before the days of refrigerators and freezers. The garden and orchard attached to the house are gradually being brought back to their well-cared for, productive state of Victorian days.

The former stables contain a blacksmith's and a wheelwright's workshop, a saddler's shop, veterinary instruments and equipment used in connection with pigs and poultry. There is also in one of the stables an introductory exhibition about farming in East Lincolnshire. The cow byre has displays relating to Lincoln Red Cattle and Lincoln Longwool Sheep.

The exhibits in the barn show the main activities of the farming year. Tools and implements used on Lincolnshire farms in the 19th century are used to illustrate the cultivation and harvesting of cereals and root crops.

In the farmyard can be seen a collection of the larger types of farm machinery. For nearly 150 years Lincolnshire has been one of the most important areas in Britain for agricultural engineering and Church Farm Museum has a number of machines, including a threshing machine by Hornsby of Grantham, a sail reaper by Edlington, of Gainsborough and a mobile cornmill by Foster of Lincoln.

Tractor-drawn implements are kept discreetly separate at the end of the orchard, so as not to interfere with the carefully created atmosphere of a Lincolnshire farm at the turn of the century.

The Parlour. Church Farm Museum, Skegness.

Museum of East Anglian Life. *Trustees. Stowmarket, Suffolk. Situated in the centre of the town. Open April 1–October 31, M.–Sa. 11–5; Su. 2–5.30.*

The Museum's growing collections are housed and exhibited in a number of buildings, in addition to the tithe barn. The open site has miraculously survived in the middle of what is now a completely built up area. At present the exhibits are accommodated in the medieval tithe barn and in the Home Close of the farm in which it stands, but a further 76 acres of farmland has been put in trust for museum use and eventually Abbot Hall itself will become part of the Museum.

Apart from what is in the tithe barn, a large part of the collections are housed and shown in a series of buildings. Some of these buildings form part of the collections, in that they have been brought to the site from elsewhere and re-erected to preserve them for future generations. So far, the Museum has five buildings of this kind: a medieval aisled hall, an 18th

century smithy from the village of Grundisburgh, and a watermill, mill house and cart lodge, dating from the 17th and 18th centuries, from Alton, near Ipswich. Just outside the Museum entrance and forming part of the Museum are two cottages in Crowe Street, built in 1709 as a single house and subsequently divided to make two separate dwellings, one of which was occupied until 1975 by the farm bailiff. The bailiff's cottage has been preserved intact with the furnishings, fittings, ornaments and domestic equipment of the last bailiff, who lived there for 40 years. The adjoining cottage has been refurbished as a farm-worker's home of 1975.

The 13th century barn, which had its thatch replaced by tiles in Victorian times, contains part of the Museum's collection of vehicles, ranging from an

Museum of East Anglian Life, Stow-market, Suffolk.

imposing estate game van to the more ordinary market and baker's carts. A number of East Anglian harvest waggons are separately housed in a building constructed specially for them. The great quantities of corn grown in this part of Britain called for massive vehicles to move it from the field to the farmstead, and the harvest waggons in this region were larger than elsewhere in Britain. A wheelwright's shop has been reconstructed at one end of this building, to show the techniques of making wooden wheels and fitting them with iron tyres.

The Engine Room, which illustrates power on the farm, is built round its largest exhibits, a steam engine of 1893, which used to drive mill machinery at Wickham Market, Suffolk. It worked for 70 years, providing flour for small local bakeries. Another modern building is devoted to the Museum's Land and Sea exhibition. East Anglia has a long coastline, which has played an important part in the lives of people settled along the coastal strip. Tourism now contributes more than fishing to their income, but where inshore fishing has survived it is interesting to see that, in striking contrast to farming, the tools and techniques have changed comparatively little over the centuries. The exhibits in the Museum's Farm Machinery section show the scale and the rate of change which have trans-formed the pattern and social context of agriculture in East Anglia probably more than anywhere else in the country.

Edgar's Farmhouse is a 14th century aisled hall – the only one so far discovered in Suffolk – which formed the inner core of a house in the village of Combs, close to Stowmarket, which had undergone con-siderable alteration and extension over the centuries. It is now used as the Museum's Education Centre. One of the bays is equipped as a school classroom of the 1920s and contains some of the furniture and equipment used in the film, *Akenfield*.

Gainsborough's House. *Gainsborough House Society. Gainsborough Street, Sudbury, Suffolk. Open Tu.–Sa. 10–12.30, 2–5; Su. 2–5.*

In 1722, John Gainsborough, father of the painter, bought two adjoining houses in Sudbury. They had both probably been built in Tudor times and one was origin-ally an inn, 'The Black Horse'. John Gainsborough had a weaving business, four children and several servants and he needed a building large enough to accommodate them all. Soon after he acquired the property, it was remodelled to make it suitable for its new purpose and the present fine Georgian front was added. It was 2 feet 2 inches longer than the previous frontages, which added threepence a year to Mr. Gainsborough's rates.

John Gainsborough was much loved in his native town, but he was not a very good businessman and in 1733 he was declared bankrupt. The family were able to con-tinue living in the house, however, through the generosity of John Gains-borough's nephew, who bought it for £500, a sum of money which made the old man's last years much easier, especially after he was given the job of Postmaster, a responsibility which was taken on by his wife after his death in 1748.

Thomas Gainsborough was born in the house in 1727 and it has been preserved as a memorial to him and his friends and contemporaries. The furniture is all of the 18th century and includes one or two items which belonged to the painter, including a colour cabinet made for his studio in London. Under the lid is a heavy slab of slate for mixing colours, and there are compartments for palette knives, brushes and dishes. The large top drawer was for storing paper and the shallow drawers underneath have compartments for dry pigments.

There are also several of Gains-borough's works – portraits of the Suffolk landed gentry, done during his years in Ipswich; portraits painted in Bath, includ-ing those of Dr. Abel Moysey, a well-respected medical practitioner in the city, and of Catherine, Countess of Dartmouth, together with one of Gainsborough's letters about it to the Earl, who was hard to please; portraits of Gainsborough's daughter; and, one of the best known of all his paintings, the group portrait in a landscape of Mr. and Mrs. Robert Andrews. The landscape this painting shows is the Andrews' estate, Auberies, outside Sudbury. What is shown of it in the painting is still recognisable today. There is also the painting of St. Mary's Church, Hadleigh, one of Gainsborough's earliest paintings and only recently rediscovered.

Gainsborough was in the habit of mak-ing models of horses, cows and dogs, which he used in the composition of his landscapes. The same animals occasion-ally reappear in different pictures. The

Period Room in Gainsborough's House. Sudbury.

Museum has the only one of these plaster casts which is known to have survived. It is of an old cart horse and it belonged at one time to John Constable.

The back of the house was altered and extended in the 1790s, to provide extra living space. The Gainsborough House Society has converted this area into a display area for exhibitions of the work of contemporary artists and craftsmen.

The garden contains a mulberry tree, which is believed to have been planted in 1610 and would certainly have been known by Gainsborough as a child. It was planted, in all probability, to provide food for the silkworms bred by an earlier occupant of the house, who may well have been a silk-weaver. John Gainsborough's weaving activities were more prosaic. He produced the material for woollen shrouds.

The East Midlands

The Gallery of Buckinghamshire Rural Life. *Buckinghamshire County Council. At the Buckinghamshire County Museum, Church Street, Aylesbury. Open M.–F. 9.30–5; Sa. 9.30–12.30 and 1.30–5.*

In Buckinghamshire, as elsewhere, the County Museum takes a broad cultural sweep across the area and presents natural history, archaeology and history. During the past hundred years, the Museum had built up a large collection of material relating to farming, rural handicrafts and village life in general. Much of this was in store and shortage of space prevented what was on display from being adequately presented. A solution was found by putting in a completely new floor at first floor level and devoting this entirely to a new Gallery of Rural Life. One of Britain's leading museum designers was engaged for the purpose and the ingenious scheme he produced has proved very satisfactory, one of the most successful facelifts to be given to a Victorian museum, within the daunting sort of budget that the ratepayers impose on local authorities.

Buckinghamshire County Museum, Aylesbury.

The aim has been to explain the life of the 19th and 20th century village in Buckinghamshire and its agricultural basis, but the scope has in fact been rather wider than this. The displays of implements and tools cover development from prehistorical cultivation to the introduction of machines in the second half of the 19th century. Dairying has been important in Buckinghamshire for more than 150 years – the nearby London market, with its insatiable demand for cheese, butter and, later, liquid milk, was the great attraction – and the Gallery pays proper attention to this. Other important displays are concerned with the specialised rural trades, such as thatching, and with the principal cottage industries, especially lace-making and straw-plaiting,

The Gallery of Buckinghamshire Rural Life. Aylesbury.

for both of which Buckinghamshire was famous.

There is a good selection of household items and an interesting, if somewhat cautious look at social life, carried out mainly by means of photographs and old documents. This includes something of the less agreeable side of rural history, its frequent poverty – before the First World War the earnings and living conditions of the Buckinghamshire farm labourer were among the worst in Britain – the under-standable unrest among agricultural workers in the 1830s, the law and its enforcement.

It is always interesting to ask a museum curator what he likes and values most in his own collections. At Aylesbury, he said:

'A working model of the Pitstone wind-mill as it was in 1800; a set of nine oil paintings by E.B. Nebot of the gardens of Hartwell House dating from the 1730s and 1740s and showing gardening practices; and a euphonicum dated 1841.'

All nice things, worth seeing and worth remembering, especially the euphonicum, an instrument which does not come one's way very often.

Waddesdon Manor. *The National Trust, Aylesbury, Buckinghamshire. Near the village of Waddesdon, on the A41, between Aylesbury and Bicester. Open March 26–October 26, W.–Su. 2–6. Good Friday and Bank Holiday Mondays 11–6. Grounds open W.–Sa. from 1, and Su. from 11.30. Closed W. after Bank Holidays.*

Between 1874 and 1889 the immensely rich Baron Ferdinand de Rothschild, of the international banking family, built himself a French Renaissance château in rural Buckinghamshire, on estates bought from the Duke of Marlborough. The

Waddesdon Manor, Aylesbury.

architect, Destailleur, was French and the gardens were laid out by another Frenchman, Lainé. The top of Lodge Hill was levelled to provide a suitable site and a light railway was constructed to bring the building materials from the Great Central Railway at Quainton, five miles away. Hundreds of mature trees were planted on the bare hillsides. Some were so large that as many as sixteen horses were needed to haul the wagons on which they were transported.

Waddesdon became one of the great English country houses. Baron Ferdinand took an active part in local affairs, as a Justice of the Peace, member of the County Council, High Sheriff and Member of Parliament for Aylesbury, a seat which was held by members of his family continuously for fifty-eight years. The Rothschilds entertained on a great scale at Waddesdon. Queen Victoria was

there and so, frequently, were King Edward VII and King George V. The visitors' book contains the signatures of five Prime Ministers.

The three members of the Rothschild family who successively inherited the estate continued the traditions of hospitality, care for the gardens and enlargement of the art collections. When James de Rothschild died in 1957, he left the property and its contents to the National Trust, as a way of fulfilling the wish of his great-uncle, Baron Ferdinand, that Waddesdon should never become unused or decayed.

During the years when the Rothschilds lived here, Waddesdon was a major centre of employment in the district, providing, at its peak, work for more than a hundred people. It is a splendidly preserved monument to a vanished way of life and full of the ghosts of departed footmen, grooms, cooks, gardeners and housemaids, a museum of social history for visitors who go round the house with the help of their imagination as well as of the guide book. But it is also one of Britain's great art museums, with the collections shown in the setting of a home, rather than a gallery.

18th century French art and furniture are particularly well represented, but there are also many fine English, Flemish and Dutch paintings and a notable collection of arms and armour.

Most of the late medieval and renaissance works of art now at Waddesdon are from the collections made by Miss Alice de Rothschild and Baron Odmond de Rothschild. They took the place of the great collections from the same period which were formed by Baron Ferdinand and which were transferred to the British Museum, as the Waddesdon Bequest, after his death in 1898.

Manor Farm Museum. *Oxfordshire County Museum Service. Cogges, near Witney, Oxfordshire. Between the B4022 and A415, close to the Witney by-pass. Open Easter Sa.–September 30, daily 11–6.*

The Manor of Cogges is mentioned in the Domesday Book. The first manor house stood close to the Windrush river and the moats which surrounded it can still be seen, although they no longer contain water. In the 13th century the De Grey

17th century wing of Manor Farm Museum, Cogges, Oxfordshire.

family, which then held the manor, built a new house on higher ground. It was modified and enlarged during the 16th and 17th centuries, but its appearance has changed very little since then. The earliest of the surviving farm buildings date from the 17th century.

The houses which formed the medieval village of Cogges have disappeared. All

108

Demonstration of hurdle-making. Manor Farm Museum, Cogges.

that now remains is the church, the tithe barn – now a school – and the Manor Farm. The present vicarage incorporates the hall of the medieval priory. Visitors to the Museum can follow an historical trail, which marks the moated manor, the medieval field systems, the priory fish-ponds and the earthworks which surround the deserted village.

In the farm buildings there are displays which follow the farming season from ploughing and sowing to harvesting. Waggons, horse-drawn implements and hand-tools show how the farmer worked and looked after his livestock a century ago. In the fully equipped Victorian dairy – the building itself is 16th century – butter is made from time to time and demonstrations of traditional rural crafts

– sheep-shearing, hurdle-making and blacksmithing – take place at weekends. There are also special days when visitors can see Shire horses and rare breeds of farm animals.

The Manor House itself has been restored and furnished to show it as it was in Edwardian times. The kitchen and back kitchen were the hall and service wing of the original 13th century house and here there are demonstrations of some of the domestic activities of 75 years ago, such as bread-making, using a bread oven, boiling laundry in a copper, and cooking on an open range.

A nice touch, very rarely to be seen in museums of this kind, is the farm pay-office, shown as it was at the beginning of the century, in the days when farm-workers received their wages entirely in coin of the realm and when ordinary people could pass their whole life without handling or seeing a banknote.

Wycombe Chair Museum. *Wycombe District Council. Castle Hill House, High Wycombe, Buckinghamshire. M., Tu., Th., F., Sa. 10–1, 2–5.*

For over 200 years, High Wycombe has been an important centre of the chair industry. The beech woods of the Chilterns provided an ample supply of excellent timber and, from its humble beginnings as a cottage craft, the industry had became very large and well organised by Victorian times. In the 1860s it was estimated that the town was producing a million and a half chairs a year, in both factories and small workshops. The reconstruction of a Windsor framer's workshop of the 1880s, with its rough bench and spoon drills, illustrates the conditions which were typical of a large part of the industry in Victorian times. An important figure for generations was the chair leg turner, known as a bodger, who worked under a thatched shelter in the woods surrounding High Wycombe. This craft was practised until the end of the

Chair leg maker at work in the woods at Prestwood, 1929. High Wycombe.

Second World War, long after the other tasks in the trade had been mechanised.

The Museum pays proper respect to the bodger, with photographs of him at work and a reconstruction of a typical workshop, complete with pole-lathe and the tools used for sawing, chopping and shaping the tree-trunks. He fits easily and naturally into the theme and atmosphere of the Museum, which is devoted to the craft, history and design of the English country-made chair, and to the development of the Windsor chair in particular. Other crafts were linked to chairmaking, including woodcarving and marquetry, but one was particularly important in High Wycombe and is represented in the Museum's displays – the caning and rushing of chair seats, which became a new source of income for women in the 1830s, when cottage-made lace became unprofitable, following the introduction of machines. Buckinghamshire lace was well-known and admired, and chair-

travellers often carried a selection of lace as well. The Museum's small lace exhibition has samples of local lace and lacemaking equipment, including some unusual bobbins.

This very attractive Museum also includes displays relating to important figures in the history of High Wycombe and the surrounding area. The Shelburne Room recalls the Earl of Shelburne (1737-1805), who lived at Wycombe Abbey and gave the Guildhall to the town. There is a portrait of him by Sir Joshua Reynolds. The Hampden Room, covering the history of the district in the 16th and 17th centuries, is named after the famous champion of civil liberties, John Hampden. It contains some interesting furniture of the Commonwealth and Restoration periods and woodcarvings by Grinling Gibbons. The 18th century is represented by a room relating to the Dashwood family of West Wycombe Park and the nineteenth by the Disraeli Room. Benjamin Disraeli lived at Hughenden Manor. There are busts of him as a young and an old man, and, to commemorate his friendship with Queen Victoria, a large portrait of the Queen by Hossborough, which dominates the room. In a somewhat minor key, the Disraeli Room also contains, among its range of Victorian exhibits, the Champion Chair, from the 1851 Exhibition, the local muffin man's bell and the leg-irons used in the local gaol.

One-arm military Windsor chairs c. 1890. Wycombe Chair Museum, High Wycombe.

Melton Carnegie Museum. *Leicestershire Museums Service. Thorpe End, Melton Mowbray, Leicestershire. Off A607, Melton to Grantham, 500 yards from centre of town. Open Easter–September 30, M.–Sa. 10–5; Su. 2–5. October 1– Easter, M.–F. 10–4.30; Sa. 10.30–4.*

The Museum sets out to present different aspects of the countryside around Melton Mowbray and to tell the visitor something about the past and present life of the area. It also functions as the local Tourist Information Centre, which is a sensible and economic way to use both staff and premises.

The method has been to divide the district into six geographical divisions and to choose, as central features of the displays, particular features of interest within each division. Melton Mowbray

Victorian Parlour. Melton Carnegie Museum, Melton Mowbray.

itself, for instance, is famous for its pork pies and Stilton cheese, but above all for its hunting. All these are included in the displays, together with a reconstruction of a middle-class parlour showing the style of life of this level of Melton society in the late 19th century.

The Vale of Belvoir, besides being prestigious hunting country, has the Grantham Canal running through it.

Many of the species of plant and animal life to be found there are shown in this part of the Museum display, together with the tools of the village wheelwright of Long Clawson, in a workshop setting. The geological area known as the Marlstone Scarp produces an extension of rocks and fossils of the Jurassic period, with an emphasis on the marlstone itself, quarried in the past for its iron content. The Belvoir Woods, man-made, were planted in the thin soil of the scarp and have their place in the Museum with an exhibition of mounted specimens of the birds which live there. The limestone plateau section is the place to show a hoard of coins and other finds from a Roman industrial site, while an exhibit dealing with the village band and friendly society of Waltham-on-the-Wolds illustrates the rural social life of more recent times.

In the River Valley area, shallow pits filled with water remind us of our present need for the beds of sand and gravel deposited during the Ice Ages. Wild duck now frequent these ponds and the different species are shown in a special display. A butcher's shop, with its full equipment, is also to be seen here. The last section, the Clay Lands, moves from the Iron Age hill fort at Burrough to the craft of the rural stonemason and from agricultural tools to a diorama of the wildlife of a typical local hedgerow.

It is an interesting, economical way of getting the flavour of a region. A set of impressions, not an encyclopaedia, is what is aimed at and the balance of long-past and almost-present and of natural and man-made help us to realise that the personality of Melton Mowbray and the surrounding countryside is not an accident. It has grown out of the soil and the climate.

Claydon House. *The National Trust. Middle Claydon, Buckinghamshire. The village is 13 miles north-west of Aylesbury and 3½ miles south-west of Winslow, off the A473. Open April 1–October 31, daily ex. M. and F., 2–6 or dusk. Open Bank Holidays, 12.30–6. Closed Good Friday and the Tuesday after Bank Holidays.*

There have been Verneys in Buckinghamshire since the 13th century and possibly even earlier, and they are known to have owned land in Middle Claydon in 1463. Sir Edmund Verney, knighted in 1611, is, however, the first to have lived here. He and his family are exceptionally well known to us from their *Memoirs*. Edited by Frances Parthenope, Lady Verney, and first published in 1892, this has become the classic portrait of the English squirearchy of the period. Sir Edmund, the most distinguished of the Verneys, was unswervingly loyal to Charles 1. He was killed at the Battle of Edgehill. When the smoke had cleared from the battle-field, there was no trace of his body, apart from his severed hand, still firmly grasping the Royal Standard.

The family suffered considerable ups and downs in their fortunes during the 18th and 19th centuries. An Irish earldom came their way, and Ralph, the improvident second Earl, began to rebuild Claydon on a colossal scale. He went bankrupt and escaped to France to avoid his creditors. His niece, who succeeded him, immediately proceeded to pull two-thirds of the house down.

Claydon House, Middle Claydon, Buckinghamshire.

Claydon House, Middle Claydon, Buckinghamshire.

In 1827 Claydon passed to a distant relation of the Verneys, Sir Harry Calvert, who took the name of Verney. He married, as his second wife, Frances Parthenope, the sister of Florence Nightingale, who often stayed at Claydon. In 1956 the family gave the house and a large part of the Park to the National Trust. Sir Ralph and Lady Verney, to whom most of the contents belong, live in the Victorianised south wing.

The rooms open to the public are distinguished especially by their astonishingly elaborate rococo decoration, much of it carried out, even on the ceilings, in carved wood. The main staircase, with the superb joinery and the delicate ironwork of the balustrade, is one of the marvels of Claydon. It was carefully restored in 1976.

Upstairs, the visitor will find almost every room is of interest, for its decoration, its furniture and its associations. They include Miss Nightingale's Room,

with its odd blend of Victorian furnishings and woodwork grained to resemble bamboo. A portrait of Florence Nightingale by W.B. Richmond hangs over the fireplace and the large photograph of her was taken in the adjoining sitting room. Near to it, the room now known as the Museum contains a variety of interesting objects with family associations, including some 17th century clothes and a number of

Opposite, above:
The Grey Drawing Room, Waddesdon Manor, Aylesbury, Buckinghamshire.
Opposite, below:
Wycombe   Chair   Museum,   High Wycombe, Buckinghamshire.

Following pages:
Left:
The Waterways Museum, Stoke Bruerne, Northamptonshire.
Right, above:
Bewdley Museum, Hereford and Worcester.
Right, below::
Carmarthen Museum, Dyfed

Florence Nightingale's letters and other memorabilia. Photographs of her taken after her return from Scutari show how thin and frail she had become as a result of the strain of organising the hospital there.

The most extraordinary room in the house is undoubtedly the Chinese Room, with its extravagant mingling of chinoiserie and rococo. The skill of the carving and the fantasy of the design are unequalled anywhere else. Most of the bamboo furniture was made in Canton c.1800 and there are also early 18th century pieces of black lacquer.

The chief interest of Claydon, perhaps, is the opportunity it provides to see how the family adapted itself to changes in its income and influence and how individual men and women of strong character succeeded in imposing their tastes and lifestyle on a house and estate which have had to endure more changes than most.

Naseby Battle and Farm Museum. *Privately owned. Purlieu Farm, Naseby, Northamptonshire. The Museum is signposted from the A50 at the junction with the B4036, and from the A508 between the villages of Maidwell and Kelmarsh. Open end of March–end of September, Sa., Su. and Bank Holidays, 2–6. Parties at other times by arrangement.*

The Museum opened in 1975 and has been created as a private venture by Mr. and Mrs. Eric Westaway and is housed in the farm where the family has lived since the end of the nineteenth century. The Battle of Naseby, which decided the outcome of the Civil War in 1645, was fought a short distance to the north of Purlieu Farm. Like all battles of the period, it was a very small-scale affair by modern standards, with thousands rather than millions of men involved, and quickly over. It was, nevertheless, a turning point in English history and it fully deserves its museum. The relics available for display are few – this was not the Somme or the Normandy beaches – but they are evocative and the imagination can do a great deal with one or two muskets and cannonballs, odd pieces of armour, a tunic button and a small collection of human bones.

At the Museum there is a large model to set the scene. Toy soldiers, accurate representations of the troops who took part in the battle, stand quietly on a relief

Opposite:
Cheddleton Flint Mill, Staffordshire.

map, while a recorded commentary describes the events and the tactics on the day when the Parliamentary army routed the Royalists. Briefed in this way, one can follow the lane towards Sibbertoft and work it all out for oneself on the actual site, thoughtfully marked with a pleasant little monument.

The men who fought at Naseby were ordinary people, temporarily and more or less willingly converted into soldiers. It is consequently very useful to have a farming museum, which is about the common man out of uniform, on the same premises as a battle museum, devoted to what the common man did when he had a musket or a pike in his hand. The peaceful part of the Museum at Purlieu Farm is housed in the old granary and in the farmyard outside. It is concerned with the objects the Victorian farmer, craftsman and housewife used as they went about their work. There are recreations of a small 19th century cottage room and scullery, where much of the collection of furnishings and household equipment is shown and exhibits of the special tools used by the rural craftsmen – the wheel-

Cottage Scullery. Naseby Battle and Farm Museum.

wright, the smith, the thatcher and others.

The outdoor exhibition in the yard centres round a carefully restored collection of vintage tractors, which, when funds permit, will have a roof over their heads.

The Waterways Museum. *British Waterways Board. Stoke Bruerne, near Towcester, Northamptonshire. From the M1 take the A508 towards Stony Stratford at Junction 15 and take the signposted turn just past the village of Roade. From the A5 take the turn marked Stoke Bruerne just south of Towcester Racecourse. Open week before Easter–mid-October, daily 10–6. Mid-October–March, Tu.–Su. 10–4.*

When the Waterways Museum was opened in 1963, the nationalised canals and river navigations had just been brought under the management of a new public body, the British Waterways Board. It was an appropriate moment to look back at Britain's canals as they had been when they occupied an important place in the nation's transport system.

The Museum building was once a grain warehouse and mill, standing by the side of the Grand Union Canal. The Grand Union linked Brentford, on the Thames, with Braunston on the Oxford Canal, and it had been built to provide a shorter route between London and the Midlands. Its construction presented great problems, but it was completed in 1800, after eight years' work, except for Blisworth Tunnel, which was not opened until 1805. Until the whole route was open, goods were taken out of the barges at Stoke Bruerne and transported up the hill to a tramway, to be reloaded into boats on the other side.

The exhibits at the Museum come from all parts of Britain and they have been arranged to present a picture of the working of the canal system and of the life of the families who operated the boats. The site is picturesque, with its humpbacked bridge, canalside inn and lock, and what is outside the Museum building forms a natural extension of what is

The Waterways Museum, Stoke Bruerne.

inside. In planning the displays, every attempt was made to satisfy both the canal fanatics, whose interest is mainly in the building and operation of the canals, and those for whom the canal people are the principal attraction, and in the result a nice balance has been kept between the two.

During the Canal Age, which lasted from about 1760 to 1840, families did not live on the boats but, when competition from the railways became fierce, the narrow-boat men cut their costs by bringing their wives and children on board to help with the crewing and to create a domestic atmosphere. The Museum has a full-sized replica of a narrow-boat cabin, decorated and furnished correctly in

every detail. One can only marvel at the ingenious way in which the boat people lived so comfortably and so tidily in such a small space. They were a closely-knit, independent-spirited community, with their own traditions and rules, and their own distinctive dress. They intermarried a great deal and they had a strict form of ceremony for the weddings, christenings and other important occasions that brought them together from time to time. The Museum documents it all and the displays will be a revelation to most people making their first visit to Stoke Bruerne.

There are a number of nice details in the technical sections, too – the apparatus for sweeping the roof of the canal tunnels, the shed in which the men employed to 'leg' boats through the tunnels used to rest and to wait for business, the gauging sticks used to determine the tonnage of cargo and therefore the toll to be paid, by measuring the depth of hull showing above the water. The measurements appropriate to each boat were decided by an elaborate procedure when it was new. Running a canal was no job for amateurs.

Wantage Museum. *Oxfordshire County Museum Service. Civic Hall, Portway, Wantage, Oxfordshire. Open W. 2–5; Sa. 10–12.30.*

This is the museum of the Vale of the White Horse, one of the oldest areas of human settlement in Britain and one of the least spoilt. The presence of early man in the area, perhaps as much as 350,000 years ago, is shown by the finds of flint tools, incorporated in the gravel beds as they were laid down at the end of the Ice Age. The bones of the animals hunted by the flint-tool makers are found in the same gravel. Excavations within the Vale of the White Horse have made it possible to trace the relationship between man and his environment from prehistoric to medieval times – his methods of hunting and farming, his food and shelter, his handicrafts, his trading pattern, his rituals and superstitions. The archaeologists have shown that, once the Roman conquest was accomplished, the chalk downs were left for the natives, while the heavier soils of the Vale came under a more intensive farming system centred on villas.

The Museum shows how the town of Wantage began as a military or trading centre in Roman times. King Alfred was born here in 849 and the area was fre-

quently invaded and looted by the Vikings. By 1086, the year of the Domesday survey, the Vale of the White Horse had become one of the most populous and prosperous parts of the region, a fortunate state of affairs which continued throughout the Middle Ages. Until the opening of the Wiltshire and Berkshire Canal in 1810, however, the economy remained on a local basis, but from then onwards farm produce from the Vale was sent to London in steadily increasing quantities, a process which was made easier by the building of the Great Western Railway and the establishment of a passenger and goods station at Wantage Road.

Wantage Museum exists to tell this story and to link it to the development of industries in the area, the tanners, the rope and sackmakers, the brewers, the ironfounders and the manufacturers of agricultural implements. There are also interesting exhibits concerning local transport, especially in the nineteenth

Opposite:
The Dairy. Wantage Museum.

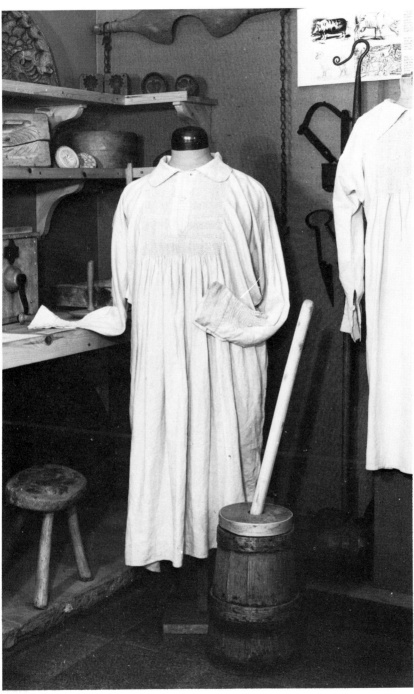

century. The canal and the railway opened up this quiet rural area to the products of industrialisation. New types of goods brought in by canal changed the economy of the town. Cheap coal started the local iron foundry and brick and tile making industries. Bricks, stone and slate became the local building materials, instead of chalk, wattle and daub. The railways changed the pattern once again. Many trades, made possible in Wantage by the canals, became unprofitable when the products of Midland factories could be brought in easily and cheaply by rail.

Wantage, a place of repeated ups and downs, is in a very real sense its own museum. The Museum itself recognises this and organises in the spring and autumn a series of guided tours, known as Wantage Walkabouts, to draw attention to what the passage of time has done to the town, often in unexpected ways. One of the problems facing the Museum's curator is the district's superabundance of history. The small museum in her care is bursting at the seams, a situation which is certain to continue until a move is made, probably in 1981, to the new Vale and Downland Centre, converted from the Old Surgery in Church Street.

The West Midlands

Bewdley Museum. *Wyre Forest District Council. Load Street, Bewdley, Hereford and Worcester. Open March 1–November 30, M.–Sa. 10–5.30; Su. 2–5.30.*

Until the end of the 18th century, Bewdley was a busy inland port on the River Severn, with close links with the Bristol merchants. The Staffordshire and Worcestershire Canal, which joined the Severn further downstream at Stourport, took away Bewdley's importance as a trading centre and, with Kidderminster then developing as the main industrial centre in the area, the town became something of a backwater and has succeeded in preserving, fortunately for the visitor, much of its 18th century appearance and charm.

The Museum is housed, very pleasantly, in the 1783 Shambles or Butchers' Market, built after the medieval market had been demolished. The Shambles consists of a central cobbled lane, with an arcade of 15 arches down each side to contain the market stalls. The market declined in the late 19th century and after the Second World War the seriously neglected buildings were acquired and restored by the Bewdley Museum Trust, which opened them as a museum in 1972.

The Museum's emphasis is on the crafts and industries which flourished in Bewdley and the Wyre Forest until comparatively recent times. The galleries have displays relating to hornmaking, capping, bark-peeling, tanning, currying, saddlery, brassware, pewtering and the craft of the wheelwright. There is also a reconstructed ropewalk and workshops of a basketmaker, cooper and blacksmith. Several craftsmen have their studios and workshops in the Museum and give demonstrations of their expertise from time to time.

A special section of the Museum, the Wyre Forest Gallery, is concerned with the crafts and industries of the Wyre Forest, particularly charcoal burning,

Basket-maker. Bewdley Museum.

basket making and besom making. The Agricultural Gallery shows the traditional activities and processes of the farming year, with a number of the larger implements displayed in the garden outside.

Before reaching these specialised galleries, visitors are given an opportunity, in an exhibition arranged in the entrance hall, to get the feeling of the district in general, and to understand something of the origins and growth of the town of Bewdley, as well as the history of the Severn, its bridges and its navigation.

In 1977 the Museum was able to buy the neighbouring brass foundry, which is now being restored to working order, before being opened to the public as an annexe to the main Museum.

Avoncroft Museum of Buildings. *Avoncroft Museum Trust. Stoke Heath, Bromsgrove, Hereford and Worcester, near the junction of the A4024 and B4091. Open March 1–November 30, daily 10.30–5.30 (or dusk, if earlier).*

Avoncroft is an open-air museum, containing a number of historic buildings from the West Midlands which have been saved from destruction, restored and re-erected on a ten-acre site. The buildings

Danzey Green Windmill. Avoncroft Museum of Buildings, Bromsgrove, Hereford and Worcester.

are very varied. They include a granary from Temple Broughton, Worcestershire; a cruck barn from Cholstry, Herefordshire; the 14th century Guesten Hall roof from Worcester, displayed at ground level; Danzey Green postmill, Warwickshire, with its wooden machinery fully restored; a 15th century timber-framed merchant's house from Bromsgrove; a

Wind-shaft and brakewheel of Danzey Post Mill. Avoncroft Museum of Buildings, Bromsgrove.

large Elizabethan house from Shrewsbury; a forge-cottage from Herefordshire; a brick octagonal counting house from Bromsgrove cattle market. There are also examples of local craft industries – a chainmaking workshop, with fourteen hearths, and a nailmaker's workshop.

Visitors to Avoncroft are usually able to see not only completed projects, but also craftsmen at work re-erecting buildings or repairing timber from buildings which have been recently rescued and brought to the site. One of the most important features of the Museum, which was opened in 1967, has been the opportunity it has provided for skilled men to work with traditional materials and structures under conditions where only the best workmanship is appropriate. At the same time, every use is made of modern methods of conservation. Avoncroft

believes that the best results are to be obtained by combining old and new skills. Sometimes, however, the old skill has to be brought back almost from oblivion. This was done, for instance, in the case of the Herefordshire barn, the restoration of which demanded both pit-sawn and split timber, and for the Bromsgrove house the panels between the structural timbers had to be made of wattle and daub, a technique which no modern building craftsman ever has occasion to practise. Avoncroft is a museum of building crafts, as well as of buildings.

Cheddleton Flint Mill. *Cheddleton Flint Mill Industrial Heritage Trust. Cheddleton, Staffordshire. 3 miles south of Leek on the A520. Open Sa. and Su. afternoons throughout the year. Parties by special arrangement at other times.*

Ground flint is used as an ingredient in the manufacture of pottery, mainly to whiten it, but also to provide the silica which makes the clay more refractory and better able to withstand high firing temperatures. Before the merits of flint were recognised in the 1720s, sand was used for the purpose, but this did not whiten the clay. When flint is ground dry, the resulting dust causes pneumoconiosis and destroys the lungs of the workers. To reduce this danger, Thomas Benson, in 1776, patented a method of grinding flint

The narrow boat Vienna, *moored by the Flint Mill Wharf at Cheddleton, Staffordshire, restored to its original 1911 appearance.*

in water. In about 1756 James Brindley produced an improved wet-grinding technique and it was this that was used in the North Mill at Cheddleton that was built by Brindley in about 1760 specially to grind flint. The South Mill was a later conversion of a corn mill.

The route of the Caldon Canal, on which Cheddleton lies, was surveyed by Brindley in 1772, the year in which he died. When the canal was opened in 1777, the transport of flint from the south-east coast via the Trent and Mersey Canal became easier and cheaper. A horse-drawn barge of the type used for carrying flint was acquired by the Museum in 1972 and, fully restored, she is now moored at the Mill wharf. This boat, the *Vienna*, was

built in Birmingham in 1911. Visitors can see how the flints were discharged straight out of the barge into the two kilns, where they were roasted before grinding.

The two water-powered mills at Cheddleton ceased operating commercially in 1963. The North Mill is now preserved much as it was built. The displays relating to the preparation of raw materials for the pottery industry are centred in and around the South Mill. The exhibits so far assembled in the South Mill include glaze and colour grinding pans, a stamp mill, edge runner mills with a frame sieve and a miller's Staffordshire cart. Water power remained important for grinding flint, stone and bone until the 1850s, but steam, first used for this purpose by Josiah Spode in 1779, was increasingly adopted by the large pottery manufacturers during the latter part of the 18th century. The Museum collections illustrate the introduction of steam for driving pottery machinery by a display built around a Robey 100 HP drop valve reciprocating steam engine, a great favourite with visitors, and a scale working model of *Old Bess*, a Newcomen engine, similar to the one installed by Spode in 1779, pumping water to an overshot waterwheel which in turn provided the power to rotate the pan for grinding the flint.

Cheddleton is the only surviving example of the water-powered grinding mill which was once characteristic of the pottery area. It has been conserved and presented in a way which makes it easy for the visitor to feel his way back into the past of an industry which has changed out of all recognition during the last 50 years.

Acton Scott Working Farm Museum. *Salop County Council. Wenlock Lodge, Acton Scott, near Church Stretton, Salop. Open March 20–October 1, M.–Sa. 1–5; Su. and Bank Holidays, 10–6.*

Acton Scott Hall was built in 1580, probably on the site of an earlier house. The Acton family, who live in the Hall today, have owned land in Acton Scott since the 13th century. At the present time, the estate covers about 1,200 acres and, of this, 22 acres and the buildings of the Home Farm form the Working Farm and the Museum. The aim has been to demonstrate life on a Shropshire mixed farm before the coming of the internal combustion engine, with horses used for all the field operations. The stock includes horses, cows, sheep, pigs and poultry of breeds rarely seen today. There is a skilled staff, but much of the work on the farm is carried out by volunteers, who give up their spare time to being trained and in this way make it possible for the traditional techniques to be passed on to

Tamworth sow. Acton Scott Working Farm Museum, Salop.

another generation.

The farmyard layout dates from 1769, but there have been later modifications and the buildings have been carefully restored by the Museum, after the last tenant farmer retired in 1974. The 1974

A swathe-turner and side delivery rake in use. Acton Scott Working Farm Museum, Church Stretton, Salop.

milking shed has been converted into a display area, to illustrate the work of the Museum. Most of the tools and equipment shown here are used during the course of the year. One milking unit has been retained, in order to allow cows to be milked according to the Dairy Hygiene Regulations and the milk to be used for butter and cheese making. Cows are still hand milked in the old cow house, but the milk has to be fed to the farm animals. In this way, visitors are able to study the great changes in dairy hygiene over the past 70 years. The Museum demonstrates butter and cheese making and production is increasing as more people become skilled in the operation of the dairy.

Most of the fields are used for grazing and for hay, but part of one meadow is ploughed, to enable a four-course rotation of winter corn, spring corn, grass or clover leys, and root or forage crops to be demonstrated. The working horses live outside all the year round, except in severe weather, but they are brought to the stables to be harnessed and groomed. The coach house forms part of the Home Farm buildings. At present, until a coach can be obtained, it is used for a display of the wheelwright's craft. A harness room adjoins the stables and a smithy has recently been added to allow a blacksmith to work on site.

Fishpools were an integral part of estate economy and management until the 19th century. Besides supplying the household with fresh fish, they provided ice for the ice house and acted as a reservoir for fire control. Over the years, most of these pools have become overgrown, but one of the two pools at Acton Scott has been restored to its original condition.

Acton Scott was the first museum of its kind in the British Isles. Its concern has always been with the quality of the visit, not with the mere number of visitors. The range of activities varies with the season, but at all times there is an opportunity for volunteers to take an active part in the Museum's work and in this way to gain a real understanding of the old farming methods.

Hereford and Worcester County Museum. *County Council of Hereford and Worcester. Hartlebury Castle, Hartlebury, near Kidderminster, Hereford and Worcester. Open February 1–November 30, M.–Th. 10–5; Sa., Su. 2–5.*

The Museum is in the north wing of the old Bishop's Palace at Hartlebury. the nucleus of the collection is the material gathered over a long period by the late Mr. and Mrs. Parker, of Bewdley, but a great deal more has been acquired since the Museum opened in 1966. Only a small proportion of the items can be shown at any one time, but the displays are changed at least once a year.

Some of the many crafts and industries of Hereford and Worcester are represented in the exhibits. They include Kidderminster carpets, Belbroughton scythes, Redditch needles, Dudley ironworking. There is an archaeological section, with material from excavations in the region, and a special collection of kitchen equipment, including an exceptionally good range of butter, cheese and marzipan moulds and an impressive 18th century spit.

A small room contains a 17th century

19th century earthenware religious ornament. Hereford and Worcester County Museum, Hartlebury.

display and on the first floor visitors can find a reproduction of a Victorian parlour and a gallery of English costume of the Victorian and Edwardian periods. A Georgian room contains furniture, porcelain, glass and costumes of the 18th and early 19th centuries. On the staircase leading up to the second floor there are two strange bedfellows, a display of contemporary Kidderminster carpets and a number of early 20th century vacuum cleaners.

Once up the stairs and safely on the second floor, the visitor is in a gallery of 19th century social life, devoted to a good slice of the activities and interests which characterised Victorian England – religion, embroidery, smoking, travel, sport, sickness, music, death, writing, marriage. At this point, at the top of the building, there is, wisely and compassionately, a

18th century shop sign from Bewdley. Hereford and Worcester County Museum, Hartlebury.

Hartlebury Castle, Hereford and Worcester County Museum.

rest area.

Having got one's second wind, one is in a proper condition to tackle the remaining collections on the top floor. There is a children's gallery, usually with as many adults as children, containing dolls' houses and toys, school books, miniature furniture and dolls made in the late 19th and early 20th centuries. Also here are displays of English coloured glass, fire plaques and old maps of Worcestershire.

Down on the ground again are a number of outside exhibits. They include a blacksmith's shop, with its forge in working order, a display of wheelwright's tools and materials, gypsy caravans, carts and farm waggons, a brougham and a hearse. As a centrepiece there is a noble cider mill, made in about 1700 and brought here from Birlingham. The grounds also include a picnic area and a nature trail.

Hartlebury Castle is remarkably good value for its modest entrance fee.

Ironbridge Gorge Museum. *Ironbridge Gorge Museum Trust. Ironbridge, Telford, Shropshire. Ironbridge is on the River Severn, on the A4169. Open April 1–October 31, daily 10–6. November 1–March 31, daily 10–5, including Bank Holidays.*

This is Britain's first open-air industrial museum or, as some prefer to call it, Britain's first industrial national park. It covers an area of six square miles along the Severn Gorge, from Coalbrookdale to Coalport, and includes a wide range of 18th and 19th century sites associated with the First Industrial Revolution, the age of coal, steam, canals and railways. It was here that the ironmaster, Abraham Darby, was the first to make a success of smelting iron with coke, in 1709. During the years which followed this pioneering development, Ironbridge was responsible for a series of important industrial firsts - the first iron rails, first iron bridge, first iron boat, first iron aqueduct, first iron steam-engine cylinders and first iron-framed building – and the River Severn was the main transport route for its raw materials and its finished products.

The Museum at Ironbridge was established in 1968 and it has grown steadily ever since. Although it is no great distance from the Black Country and the Potteries, with the new town of Telford butting up against its northern edge, it preserves much of its original rural flavour. It is 18th century industry, with trees and a river, and Ironbridge itself is more of a village than a town. Only the very lazy and those with small children drive from one part of the Museum to another. Those who walk gain a lot.

The original 1709 furnace, perhaps the most important industrial shrine in the world, was excavated and restored in 1959 by Allied Ironfounders, the successors to the Coalbrookdale Company established by Abraham Darby. It was opened to the public, together with a small museum, on the 250th anniversary of Darby's successful experiments. The furnace and museum, which contains a selection of the products of the works during its long history, now forms part of Ironbridge Gorge Museum.

To this have been added and restored over the past ten years a number of buildings which illustrate the industrial development of the area – the Severn Warehouse, built by the Coalbrookdale Company in the 1840s and now the home of the Museum's introductory exhibition to the Gorge and Telford (the man and the town); the Iron Bridge, cast at Coalbrookdale in 1779; the bridge tollhouse, now an information and exhibition centre; the two Bedlam furnaces, constructed in 1757; and the Coalport China Works Museum, where china was made until 1926, when the company moved to Staffordshire. The old works have now been restored and adapted as a museum of Coalport – its

techniques of manufacture, its products and the people who worked there. The most recent project has been the transformation of the Great Warehouse at Coalbrookdale into a Museum of Iron, which traces the use of the metal from the earliest times down to the mid-19th century.

Two other important parts of the Museum relate to the same themes and the same period as the restored buildings, but they are industrial history and archaeology of a different kind. Blists Hill Open Air Museum is a 42-acre woodland site on which are being recreated the historic Shropshire industries of iron, coal and clay, together with early transport systems and a reconstructed toll-cottage, with Victorian furniture and domestic equipment. The site includes the Hay Inclined Plane, which took barges down from the Shropshire Canal to the Severn. And, to set the seal on the Museum's long series of achievements, the magnificent collection, 'Images of the Industrial Revolution', formed by the late Sir Arthur Elton from the time he was fifteen until his death in 1974, is now displayed in the Coach House Gallery. Jigsaw puzzles, handkerchiefs, cups and saucers, paintings and drawings, everything, great and small, which showed the extent to which the Industrial Revolution had entered the minds and emotions of the British people is here in the Elton Collection.

Opposite:
Steam Winding Engine. Blists Hill Open Air Museum, Ironbridge.

THE STUDY, ELGAR'S BIRTHPLACE

Elgar's Birthplace. *The Elgar Birthplace Trust and its Foundation. Lower Broadheath, near Worcester, Hereford & Worcester. The Broadheath turning is off the A44, 2 miles from Worcester in the direction of Leominster. Open weekdays, except W., May 1–September 30, 1.30–6.30. October 1–April 30, 1.30–4.30. Bank Holidays 10.30–12.30, 1.30–4.30.*

Sir Edward Elgar was born at Broadheath in 1857, in a pleasant, double-fronted brick cottage overlooking the Malvern Hills. After his death in 1934, the cottage was bought by Worcester Corporation, as a memorial to the composer's life and work, and since 1936 it has been maintained as a museum by the Birthplace Trust, helped in recent years by funds raised by the Elgar Foundation.

The modest but much-visited museum now houses a collection of memorabilia of Elgar and his work. They include photographs, programmes, scrapbooks and personal possessions and, as one of the Museum's most valued possessions, the manuscript scores of his Second Symphony and String Quartet. There are also a number of items of furniture belonging to Elgar, his desk among them. Until

The Study. Elgar's Birthplace, Lower Broadheath.

recently, only three rooms were available for display purposes, since the Curator lived on the premises, but the success of the Foundation's fund-raising activities has made it possible to provide alternative living accommodation elsewhere and in this way to extend the Museum area considerably, a welcome development, since gifts of interesting material connected with Elgar are constantly made to the Trust, which has been embarrassed and frustrated by having nowhere to show them.

Elgar's biographer, Michael Kennedy, has pointed out the strange fact that, although the composer spent only the first two years of his life in the cottage of

Broadheath, 'by some extrordinary alchemy, it is redolent of Elgar'. Partly by luck and partly by judgement, the mementoes are there in just the right number and proportion to stimulate the imagination, without, as many of the museums devoted to the great succeed in doing, overwhelming and anaesthetising it.

Ludlow Museum. *Salop County Council. Butter Cross, Ludlow, Shropshire. Open Easter–September 30, M.–Sa. 10.30–12.30, 2–5. June 1–August 31, also Su. 10–1, 2–5.*

Ludlow Museum has romantic origins. Early in the 19th century, Lucien Bonaparte, the brother of Napoleon, was taken prisoner. The ever-considerate British put a large house in Ludlow at his disposal for as long as he was obliged to stay in England. To help pass the time, he formed a museum in the outbuildings, and when he returned to France in 1811, he left part of his collection behind to form the nucleus of the proposed town museum. Matters proceeded somewhat slowly, but in 1833 the museum was at last founded by the Ludlow Natural History Society, of which the geologist, Sir Roderick Murchison, and other eminent men of science, were members. The collections grew rapidly, mainly as a result of gifts, and a century later their display was presenting considerable problems. In 1955 a mid-18th century building, the Butter Cross, became the

Ludlow Museum, Salop.

134

STAFFORDSHIRE COUNTY MUSEUM

Museum's display area, the scientific study collections being kept elsewhere in the town. The Museum is now part of the County Museum Service.

The Prehistory Section contains good Stone Age and Bronze Age material. Many of the exhibits have been found by children, an outstanding example being an early Bronze Age flat axe, discovered by a Ludlow schoolboy. The years of the Roman occupation are well represented, a particular attraction being the finds from Leintwardine, the Roman Bravonium. These include part of the hypocaust, with a dog's footprint on one of the tiles.

The real history of Ludlow begins at the end of the 11th century, with the building of the Castle Keep. In medieval times the walled town became an important centre of the wool trade and its prosperity continued until the 17th century. Life during this period is well illustrated in the displays, the exhibits including an unpleasant iron mask, discovered in the Castle well, which was used for compressing a victim's skull. By the time of the Georges, the

Castle had become an uninhabited ruin and Ludlow was no longer a place of any importance, except as a residential centre, a situation which continued throughout the reign of Victoria and which allowed Ludlow to escape the usual fate of Victorian rebuilding. The displays reflecting life in the 18th and 19th centuries are consequently of a mainly peaceful and domestic nature – household equipment, playbills, coaching notices, costumes, a doll's house, toys.

The area is important geologically and the links with the original Natural History Society are preserved by displays of fossils, rocks and minerals and by habitat groups of plants and wild creatures.

Ludlow, as a result of the good fortune of having been a backwater during the period of the Industrial Revolution and Victorian prosperity, is still a town of real charm. Nothing illustrates this better than the Museum's collection of the delightful watercolours of Ludlow by Louise Rayner, which capture the spirit of the place to perfection.

Staffordshire County Museum. *Staffordshire County Museum Service. Shugborough, Staffordshire. Car access is from Milford, on the A513, 6 miles east of Stafford. The nearest M6 interchanges are 13 (south) and 14 (north). Open mid-March–mid-October, House and Museum, Tu.–F. 10.30–5.30; Sa., Su., Bank Holidays, 2–6. Farm, Sa., Su., Bank Holidays, 2–6 and, for parties only, by appointment during the week. Mid-October–mid-March, Museum Tu.– F. 10.30–4.30, 1st and 3rd Su. in each month, 2–4.30. House open by appointment to parties only during these months. Farm closed during the winter.*

Until the Reformation, Shugborough belonged to the Bishops of Lichfield. It passed into the hands of the Anson family in 1624. In 1693 the first block of a new house was built on the site, the old house having been demolished, and this was greatly extended and improved during the following century by Thomas Anson, who succeeded to the property in 1720,

with the help of his much richer younger brother, George, First Lord of the Admiralty, who was created Lord Anson in 1747. When the Admiral died in 1762, Thomas Anson inherited his considerable fortune and all his possessions and this resulted in further improvements to the estate. During the 19th century, the Ansons became Earls of Lichfield. The

*Staffordshire County Museum, Shug-
borough.*

present Earl continues to live in part of
the house, which now belongs to the
National Trust. The Museum and the
estate are administered by Staffordshire
County Council.

The house, much of which is accessible
to visitors, contains fine collections of
17th, 18th and early 19th century furniture and paintings, including many family
portraits. The garden buildings are
impressive. Among them is the Chinese
House, completed in 1747, soon after
Admiral Anson's return from a voyage
round the world, which had included a
long stay at Canton, and the Cat's Monument, erected as a memorial to Thomas
Anson's Siamese cat, a rare breed in
Britain at that time.

In the former domestic buildings of the
house, the brewhouse, laundry and coachhouses have been restored and are presented, with their original equipment, as
they looked in Victorian times. There are
also exhibitions of domestic life, costume,
traditional and contemporary crafts and
agriculture. The emphasis in the Museum
is on rural life, since the major manufacturing towns of Staffordshire have
their own specialist museums, and the
domestic exhibits are concerned with the
county's history as a whole, not merely

with stately homes. But the Shugborough laundry and brewery inevitably steal much of the show. The laundry, fully equipped in the Victorian fashion, was in operation between the 1780s and 1930s, the ironing room was originally on the first floor but has now been reconstructed near the laundry on level ground. The laundry work took the whole week, from Monday to Saturday. The Shugborough brewhouse provided beer for the staff in the house at an allowance which works out at an average of a gallon each for every day in the year. Brewing took place once a month.

The galleries at the Museum at Shugborough are installed in rooms on the first floor of the house, where the maids' bedrooms once were. They cover a number of interesting themes usually neglected by museums devoted to country life – land drainage, hedging, timber-felling, millstone dressing and veterinary work.

The Museum has a fine collection of horse-drawn vehicles used for both town and country transport. The small selection displayed in the coachhouses at Shugborough are mostly examples of vehicles belonging to the farms and country estates. All of them have strong Staffordshire county connections.

A quarter of a mile from the house and museum is Shugborough Park Farm, which was built c.1800 as the home farm of the estate. It has been restored and

The Chinese House. Staffordshire County Museum, Shugborough.

stocked as a museum of agriculture, with displays of farm machinery and local breeds of livestock – Longhorn and White Park cattle, Shropshire sheep, Tamworth pigs, Bagot goats, Derbyshire Redcap fowls and Old English game. The farm buildings, designed by Samuel Wyatt, were completed more or less in their present form, by 1805. They include, in addition to the farmhouse itself, the granary, cornmill, stabling, cattle-sheds and implement housing.

Shugborough is still collecting and still growing. As with all museums, the main concern is necessarily with objects, but there are also extensive collectons of what the Museum calls 'background material' – sales notices, instruction manuals, catalogues and photographs, as well as recorded reminiscences of craft techniques, special events, schooldays and life in domestic service.

Wales

Abergavenny Museum. *Monmouth District Council's Museum Service. The Castle, Castle Street, Abergavenny, Gwent. Open March 1–October 31, M.–Sa. 11–1, 2–5 and Su. 2.30–5; November 1–February 28, M.–Sa. 11–1, 2–4; closed Su.*

The Museum is situated in the grounds of the ruined castle on the south-west side of the town. The building is interesting, an early 19th century dwelling house and hunting lodge constructed on top of a 12th century motte and bailey. Over the centuries the Norman castle has been the setting of bloody events, such as the 1175 massacre of the Welsh chieftains of Gwent, which were normal in this ferocious border country. What remains of the castle now is only a poor survival of its former grandeur, but it provides a distinguished and stimulating background to the Museum, which was set up in 1959 on

the initiative of a group of local people, who formed themselves into the Abergavenny Museum Society, and was transferred to the care of the new Monmouth Council in 1974.

The emphasis is on local life in the 19th and early 20th centuries, the period of the Welsh cultural revival. Today Abergavenny is a busy market town, but both the town and the surrounding countryside have seen great changes since the death of Queen Victoria and during the upheavals caused by two World Wars and the growth of modern-type industrialisation and agriculture. One of the Museum's most important tasks has been to document the age of self-sufficiency, when

Welsh Kitchen. Abergavenny Museum.

every local home made its own bread, cheese and butter and every town and village had its own craftsmen to serve the community. The 19th century border kitchen is one of the most attractive features, closely rivalled by the saddler's shop, which is entirely fitted out with the tools and products of the Abergavenny saddler, Russell Williams.

The town's heyday as a tourist resort is well-remembered. 'Pleasantly situate on the banks of the Usk,' it presented, said its Victorian publicists, 'unusual advantages to health and pleasure seekers', with everything the heart of a walker, a fisherman or an idler could possibly desire. Equally distinguished amenities were at the service of 'the Invalid and Dyspeptic'. From massacres to cheesemaking and from saddlers to mineral springs, Abergavenny has had much to offer and its Museum shows us an excellent selection.

Ceredigion Museum. *Ceredigion District Council. 14 Vulcan Street, Aberystwyth, Dyfed. Open M.–Sa. 2–6.*

Ceredigion is still known to most people outside Wales as Cardiganshire and the museum at Aberystwyth is the only one to

Bedroom. Ceredigion Museum, Aberystwyth.

cover the county as a whole. It was opened in 1973 in a pleasant Georgian terrace house at one time occupied by a sea-captain, a reminder of the days when the town was a base for the overseas trade of North and Central Wales. Ceredigion

Museum has some interesting seafaring displays.

The traditional way of life of the region is presented through displays of the tools, implements, furniture and domestic equipment used in the past. Owing to its somewhat remote position, Ceredigion has preserved more of the old customs and practices than other parts of Wales. The use of wooden bowls, plates and spoons, for instance, can still be found occasionally, with the 'fire on the floor', where cooking is carried out in cauldrons and baking pots. They are to be seen in one of the Museum's most popular exhibits, the reconstruction of a one-roomed cottage as it was in about 1850.

Wales and sheep are inseparable. Sheep are the only crop, apart from grass, that many of the moors and hillsides can grow and without them the homesteads and cottages of Ceredigion would have lacked their most appreciated food and the principal source of their textiles. The Museum pays a proper tribute to the all-important sheep and to the craftsmen and craftswomen who turned them to human use. The demonstrations of spinning are greatly appreciated by visitors and have the added advantage of encouraging the spinning ladies and keeping them in regular practice, at a time when the woollen industry has almost gone from the area. Fifty years ago there were more than sixty woollen mills in Ceredigion; now only four remain.

The northern part of Ceredigion is rich in lead ore, and the remains of over two hundred mines and workings are dotted about the county, evidence of a local industry which was important for nearly two thousand years. Lead, too, has its proper place in the Museum, as part of the panorama of the variety of Ceredigion life through the ages, certain details of which the uninformed tourist might well not have suspected.

Museum of Welsh Antiquities. *University College of North Wales. Next to the main bus station. Ffordd Gwynedd, Bangor, Gwynedd. Open M.–Sa., 10.30–4.30.*

The Museum was first established in 1884, as part of the University College of North Wales, but it incorporated an earlier collection. After nearly a century on College premises, which in Bangor are not exactly conveniently placed for the casual visitor, the decision was made, in 1973, to move down to the city, close to the Old Canonry, where an Art Gallery had already been established. The change proved to be very wise. The increase in attendance figures was large and immediate, especially as the local authority provided no direction signs.

The Museum is concerned mostly with exhibits from North Wales. It has a notable collection of 17th, 18th and 19th century furniture, two particularly good displays illustrating the interior of a typical farmhouse kitchen and a Caernarvonshire country house.

There are special displays of Welsh crafts and industries, especially slate quarrying and slate dressing, textiles and fishing. Costumes and samplers, mainly from the Victorian period, blend agreeably with the furniture and introduce some welcome touches of colour. Welsh furniture is nearly all made of oak and its dark tones present the museum curator with the problem of avoiding an atmosphere of overall gloom, especially when the floors are of the same dark oak as the furniture. The white walls of the Museum

Museum of Welsh Antiquities, Bangor.

galleries help considerably in this and the black and white effect is very pleasing. A little relief does no harm, however, and the Museum is the fortunate possessor of a good deal of excellent pottery and porcelain, which are strategically and fairly generously placed, with satisfying visual results.

Two other features of the Museum call for special mention. The first is a fine display from the Cyrig Lwyd stone axe factory, one of the most important pre-historic centres in Britain for stone implements, and the second is the group of exhibits relating to the pair of great bridges across the Menai Straits, Telford's road bridge and Stephenson's Britannia rail bridge. These are attractively described by means of models and old prints. The Museum is blessed, by the way, with a very good print room.

The Honorary Curator describes this as 'one of the few straight museums in North Wales' and, in these reprehensible days of gimmicks and a philosophy of 'get-the-numbers-at-all-costs', one understands what he means.

Welsh Folk Museum. *National Museum of Wales. St. Fagans, Cardiff. Open October–March, M.–Sa. 10–5; Su. 2.30–5. April–September, M.–Sa. 10–6; Su. 2.30–6. Closed Christmas Eve, Christmas Day, Boxing Day, New Year's Day, May 1.*

The Museum lies to the west of Cardiff, within the fork formed by the A4119 and A48. It was established in 1948, in the buildings, formal gardens and park of St. Fagans Castle, formerly the home of the Earl of Plymouth. The aim from the beginning has been to create a centre which would illustrate the development of the domestic, social and cultural life of Wales over a period of several hundred years. The museum resulting from this policy falls into two parts, a main block housing the Galleries of Material Culture, Costume, Agriculture and Agricultural Vehicles, and a number of houses and workshops brought from different parts of Wales and re-erected at various points within the Museum's 100-acre site.

The Material Culture Gallery contains a comprehensive collection of furniture and domestic equipment of all kinds, as well as displays concerned with civil life and the maintenance of law and order. The Folklore section has wassail bowls, valentines, and a fine range of love spoons. Musical instruments are well

A hay barn from N. Wales in the course of re-erection at the Welsh Folk Museum, Cardiff.

represented and the Eisteddfod and Gorsedd material includes medals, crowns, chairs and regalia from 1789 to the present day. Religion, education, games, Friendly and Temperance Societies, and medicine are all represented in this Gallery, and very few visitors will fail to note the exhibit relating to Dr. William Price, the pioneer of cremation.

The Costume Gallery shows the different styles of dress and accessories worn in Wales during the past 250 years. The Gallery emphasises the close links which can be observed, decade by decade, between the design of costume, furniture and interior decoration. The items in the Agriculture and Agricultural Vehicles Galleries cover a period of more than two

View of the coracles in the Net House, Welsh Folk Museum, Cardiff.

centuries, from the simplest hand-tools to tractors and from hand-drawn sledges to four-wheeled waggons of great beauty and elegance. There is a special section dealing with the care and management of livestock.

The seventeen individual buildings so far installed in the grounds of the Museum have been carefully chosen to illustrate the varied pattern of rural activity – different types of farmhouse, cottage and mill, a tollhouse, a tannery, a smithy, a cockpit, a Unitarian chapel, a gypsy caravan, a boat and net-house. The buildings are appropriately furnished and equipped and there are regular demonstrations by a blacksmith, wood-turner and other craftsmen.

St. Fagans Castle – Castle is a misnomer – itself is preserved and shown in its own right, as a separate feature of the Museum. Built in 1570, it is a good example of the many-gabled Elizabethan style and contains a large collection of 17th–19th century furniture, tapestries and pictures, including portraits of the Plymouth family, who owned St. Fagans from 1730 to 1947.

Handloom at the Esgair Moel Woollen Factory (built c. 1760). Welsh Folk Museum, Cardiff.

Carmarthen Museum. *Dyfed County Council. Abergwili, Carmarthen, Dyfed. Open M.–Sa. 10–4.30.*

The new Carmarthen Museum was opened in 1978, in what was formerly the Palace of the Bishop of St. David's, two miles east of Carmarthen on the A40. The original museum was founded by the Carmarthenshire Antiquarian Society in 1905 and was housed in Quay Street, Carmarthen.

The seven acres of grounds surrounding the Museum formed part of the garden of the Bishop's Palace. They contain an interesting variety of trees and shrubs and have fine views of the lower Towy Valley. A Nature Trail in the grounds provides the visitor with a survey of the natural history of the area and this is backed up by an exhibition in the Interpretation Room in the Old Lodge.

The main gallery in the Museum illustrates the archaeology and history of the Carmarthen region. The archaeological material is particularly good. It includes the Roman gold pendant and chain found near the gold mines at Dolaucothi, near Pumsaint. The collection of inscribed standing stones is also on display in this gallery. The Ceramics Gallery has delightful pottery from the Llanelly and Swansea potteries and the Dairy displays traditional butter and cheese making equipment from the Carmarthen region. The other galleries are devoted to Folk Life, Costume and Natural History.

In the foyer of the Museum is the frieze from the original Picton Monument at Carmarthen. General Sir Thomas Picton, born in Pembrokeshire, died leading his troops in a charge at Waterloo and the Monument commemorates the heroic scene in proper detail. With its scenes of battle, blood and death, one is a long way from the butter churns, the oak dressers and the frolics of the Llanelly plates. But the general tone of the Museum is of Welsh kitchens, dresses, farmyards and wildlife, not of death and slaughter, although the area has had its fair share of that in days gone by.

Chepstow Museum. *Monmouth District Council. Bridge Street, Chepstow, Gwent. Open March 1–October 31, daily 2–5.*

Chepstow grew up around its castle, strategically situated near the point where the Wye joins the Severn. Until the end of the 19th century, it was a flourishing port and market town. With easy access to timber, Chepstow was an ideal place to build wooden ships and during the 1880s

The Board School. Chepstow Museum, Gwent.

and 1890s the yards moved over to the construction of iron ships. They now concentrate on heavy engineering work, much of it bridge building.

Chepstow Museum was founded in 1949 by the Chepstow Society and run for the next quarter of a century entirely by volunteers. By 1976, however, the financial and administrative commitment had become too great and the District Council

Stone Cross c. 11th century, Chepstow Museum.

immediate surroundings, its castle, ships and port, wine trade, agriculture, domestic and social life, commerce and entertainments.

The great charm of a museum created by a local society is usually the broad sweep that it takes across the past of its area, and Chepstow is no exception to the rule. The past of Chepstow, illustrated in museum terms, includes, in no particular order of priority, a number of good 18th and 19th century clocks made in the town, domestic Victoriana connected with local families, a double cheese press, hundreds of old postcards, a penny farthing bicycle, letters, plans, pictures and tools relating to Brunel's Bridge and the Shipyard, and a 'Junior Expert' gramophone of 1930, with a 2-foot diameter horn, which is in excellent working order and plays 78s for the pleasure of visitors.

This approach to local history may be called impressionistic or untidy, according to one's point of view. But much of the pleasure of history lies in its essential untidiness, which a museum like Chepstow reflects very faithfully, to the obvious satisfaction of most of the people who come to see it.

absorbed the Museum into its newly formed museum service. For some years after it was established, the Museum was housed in the medieval Town Gate, but it eventually outgrew these premises and moved into the old Board School for Girls, where it has remained ever since.

The Museum takes note of the fact that it lies at the beginning of the Wye Valley, one of the most visited areas in Britain. It has a fine collection of prints and water-colours of the Wye Valley and Tintern Abbey, from the 18th century onwards, which provide an interesting opportunity to compare the way in which artists have seen the same views at different periods. Most of the collections, however, have to do with the history of Chepstow and its

Scrimshaw work carved from a whale tooth. Chepstow Museum.
Opposite:
North Wales Quarrying Museum, Llanberis, Gwynedd.

Museum of the Woollen Industry. *National Museum of Wales: Welsh Folk Museum. Dre-fach Felindre, Dyfed, close to the junction of the A484 and B4334. Open April–September, M.–Sa. 10–5.*

The Museum, established in part of a working mill, was opened in 1976. It is concerned with the interpretation of the most extensive of the Welsh rural industries. From 1860 to 1930, the villages of the middle Teifi Valley and Dre-fach Felindre in particular, were the most important woollen manufacturing centres in Wales. Nowadays it is nearly all industrial archaeology, with most of the old mills shut and derelict. Some never progressed beyond waterpower, some moved into the steam age. Within a mile of the Museum, all the stages in the evolution of the woollen industry can be seen. The local rivers are swift-flowing and there was a good supply of power at all times of the year, so good that everybody wanted it, and in 1899 one observer noted that 'there is hardly a place on the banks of the rivers where it would be convenient to build another factory or mill'. The Museum has set up a Factory Trail, so that visitors can plot the growth and decay of the industry for themselves.

Above:
The Museum of the Woollen Industry, Dre-fach Felindre, Dyfed.

Opposite, above:
Higher Mill Museum, Helmshore, Lancashire.
Opposite, below:
'The Grove' Rural Life Museum, Ramsey, Isle of Man.

The Museum falls into two parts. First, there is an exhibition of photographs, machinery and equipment that traces the development of the Welsh woollen industry from the Middles Ages to the present day, and, second, an exhibition of the products of some of the present-day mills, arranged in the manner of a commercial showroom. The visitor will find a good collection of the tools and machines which have been used for the carding and spinning of wool and the warping, weaving and finishing of the cloth, with the various processes clearly explained.

The task of blending ancient and modern, and of telling the story of change and decay on the one hand and present-day enterprise on the other is a difficult one, but it has been skilfully accomplished. The Museum of the Woollen Industry is an interesting illustration of a new and very welcome trend, which tries to abolish the traditional distinction between a museum and an exhibition, between past and present. The old fear of being attacked for spending rates and taxes on publicising commercial firms and their products is gradually disappearing and the public is having a more interesting and rewarding time as a result.

North Wales Quarrying Museum. *Department of the Environment and National Museum of Wales. Gilfach Ddu, Llanberis, Gwynedd. Open Easter–Spring Bank Holiday, daily 9.30–5. Spring Bank Holiday–September 30, daily 9.30–7. During winter months the Museum is open to groups by special arrangement.*

The Museum is housed in the former Dinorwic Quarry workshops, a majestic group of buildings which lie near Llyn Padarn Lake, east of Llanberis. It is reached by means of a side road branching off the main A4086, almost immediately opposite the Snowdon Mountain Railway.

The ownership and organisation of the Museum are somewhat complicated. When the quarry closed in 1969, the workshops were bought by what is now the Gwynedd County Council. The buildings were placed under the guardianship of the Secretary of State for Wales and are now maintained by the Department of the Environment on his behalf. The displays in the Museum have been arranged by the National Museum of Wales and the engine sheds are leased by the County Council to the private company which runs the lakeside railway.

Slate quarrying in North Wales dates from the end of the 18th century. Two methods of working were developed: underground mining, as at Blaenau Ffestiniog, and terraced open quarrying, covering the whole slope of the mountain, as at Dinorwic. By the end of the 19th century, 3,000 people were working at Dinorwic, blasting, transporting, sawing and splitting the slate. The end product

Above:
Splitting slates, North Wales Quarrying Museum, Llanberis.
Opposite:
North Wales Quarrying Museum, Llanberis.

was roofing slates, for which there was a great demand, both in Britain and overseas. The work was dangerous and casualties were frequent. To deal with injuries, a special company hospital was built not far from the quarry. It has been closed for many years, but a special exhibition devoted to it, including examples of the medical and surgical equipment, has been created in the Museum.

It was essential for such a large industrial enterprise in a remote location to have its own workshops. These were on an impressive scale, built of granite around a central courtyard. Power for the machinery came from an enormous waterwheel, over 50 feet in diameter and with an axle a foot thick. The workshops were equipped for woodworking, pattern-making, foundry work, metal-working, fitting and erecting, and much of the original machinery remains in place.

Most of what was formerly the smithy has been transformed into an exhibition area, which illustrates the finishing end of the quarry, including the sawing of the blocks into slabs and the splitting and dressing to size of the slates. From time to time there are demonstrations of the highly skilled arts of splitting and trimming. The exhibition also shows, by means of films, slides and display panels, how work at the quarry was organised and carried out and how it fitted into the life of the district. There is a great deal of information about the neighbouring villages and their people, politics, strikes and lockouts, leisure activities, the chapels and the eisteddfods. Every effort has been made to make sure that the visitor becomes acquainted with the men who worked at Dinorwic, and who were often injured and killed there, during a period of nearly two centuries, and not merely with the machinery and tools with which they made a living for themselves and profits for their employers.

This is very much the new style of technical and industrial museum, with the added advantage of being in the middle of some of Britain's finest scenery.

Newtown Textile Museum. *Newtown Textile Museum Society. 5–7 Commercial Street, Newtown, Powys. Open April 1–October 31, Tu.–Sa. 2–4.30. Mornings by application to caretaker at 7 Commercial Street.*

During the last decade of the 18th century, Newtown began to develop as an important centre of the woollen industry, producing Welsh flannel of the highest quality. The first phase of the industry, based on the handloom, reached its peak in the 1830s, by which time the population of the town had more than quadrupled in thirty years. During the Forties and Fifties, the industry was in a depressed state, but steam-powered machinery was introduced in the 1860s and during the next thirty years there was a welcome but, as it proved, temporary return to prosperity. Another decline set in at the beginning of the 1890s and from this there was no real recovery. The last of Newtown's woollen mills closed down in 1935.

In 1962 a committee was formed to explore the possibilities of setting up a museum which would look back to the time when Newtown was the Leeds of Wales. The committee was eventually able to acquire one of the composite buildings which, in the days of the handloom weavers, were half living accommodation, half workshop. The weaving floor ran along the top of Nos. 5–7 Commercial Street and was shared by the various

The Carding and Spinning Room. Newtown Textile Museum.

families living on the floors below. In the former weaving rooms there is now a museum which tells the story of Newtown's industrial past and also illustrates its social history during the 18th and 19th centuries.

Two handlooms have been installed, together with other tools and equipment once used in the industry, including an example of the original type of Welsh Great Wheel, used for spinning. All the processes, from the raw wool to the finished product, are explained, and there is an exhibit likely to be welcomed by visitors not previously familiar with these matters which demonstrates in a clear and simple fashion the different kinds of wool produced by different breeds of sheep.

There is an exhibition of woollen fabrics made in Newtown and elsewhere in Wales yesterday and today, a pleasant reassurance that the old craftsmanship and traditions are by no means dead and that there is still a good market for textiles made in small workshops, provided the designs are acceptable.

This is not a professional museum, but it is arranged with great charm and run with enthusiasm. It gains enormously from being in a building which is full of the ghosts of long-dead handloom weavers and their families.

The Welsh Miners Museum. *Welsh Miners Museum Committee. Afan Argoed Country Park, Cynonville, Port Talbot, West Glamorgan. On the A4107, Port Talbot to Treorchy. Open Easter–September 30, 10.30–6.30. October 1– Easter, Sa., Su. 12–5.*

To those unfamiliar with Wales, there may seem something odd about the idea of a mining museum in a country park, but in fact mining here was for a very long time a rural activity, with mines opened up all along the valleys in the midst of what was, and for the most part still is, some of the finest scenery in Britain. If there had been no waste tips and if metal-working had not

Underground road with tram. The Welsh Miners Museum, Port Talbot.

been established close to the coal mines in some areas, especially near the coast of South Wales, the mining industry would have brought little change to the landscape, since most of its activity is hidden away underground. As it is, with the mines closed and the waste heaps concealed under carefully planted woodland, one could very well drive up the valley to the Museum from Port Talbot now without having any idea that this had been until comparatively recently an important

centre of the coal industry. The last pit to operate in the Afan Valley only closed, in fact, in 1970.

The communities in the Valley had come into existence to mine coal and, with mining no longer a means of livelihood for local people, a very broadly based committee, including a number of retired miners, was formed to create a museum in which the story of the miners and their families could be told. The name of the museum which resulted was, it should be noted, the Welsh Miners Museum, not the Welsh Mining Museum. Opened in 1976, as a joint enterprise of the Museum Committee, the County Council and the Countryside Commission, the Museum forms part of a complex of buildings which also includes a Countryside Centre. In it, by entering simulated coal faces, looking at underground and above-ground equipment and studying photographs, documents and dioramas, the visitor can experience something of the realities of coal-getting and understand the effect it

The Welsh Miners Museum, Port Talbot, West Glamorgan.

had on the communities of South Wales, with their chapels, hymn-singing, Penny Readings, Miners' Institutes and well-patronised public houses.

The planning of the Museum, the building up of the very fine collections and the construction of the exhibits has been a community project, carried out to a great extent by volunteers. Many of the photographs, documents and objects on display have come from mining families and from the Union. Health, living conditions, safety measures, political activity, trade unionism and strikes all have their sections of this well-arranged Museum, which contrives to fit a remarkable number of exhibits into a relatively small space. No-one, surely, could go round it without a feeling of admiration and gratitude for the men who faced such gruelling working conditions and faced such terrible risks, generation after generation.

Some of the photographs and documents, especially from the 1920s and 1930s, are so shocking as to have the appearance of coming from another planet rather than merely another age.

Yet, unbelievably, it is a museum completely without recrimination or bitterness. The mining families who created it have been content to let the facts speak for themselves.

Erddig. *The National Trust, Wrexham, Clwyd. One mile south of Wrexham, off A483. Open April 4–October 26. Tu.–Su. 12–5.30. Also Bank Holiday M., 12–5.30. Agricultural Museum, July 5–October 26.*

Erddig is no ordinary country house, either in its history or in its presentation as a National Trust property. It belonged to a family who were uncommonly kind to their servants, and visitors nowadays enter it from the working side, not through the front door. It is the first of the National Trust's houses to be interpreted from the point of view of the servants quite as much as from that of the owners and it may well represent the beginnings of a fundamental change of policy, although not all country houses, of course, are equally well suited to such democratic treatment.

Built in the 1680s, added to in the 1720s and refaced in the 1770s, Erddig is not by any means an architectural masterpiece, but it is a friendly, interesting place, with a lot of good eighteenth century furniture, portraits, porcelain and musical instruments and an unusually complete range of workshops, domestic offices and outbuildings, which provide an exceptionally good opportunity to see how the self-contained English country estate worked. One of its most remarkable features, which makes it much more than a mere assembly of rooms and furniture, is the series of portraits of the household and estate servants, with accompanying verses, which was begun in the late 18th century and continued well into the 19th. In most houses, the servants play no part in the historical record, but Erddig is refreshingly different.

The Yorke family acquired the property in 1733 and they continued to own it until 1973, when the last Squire, Philip Yorke – the head of the family was always Philip or Simon – gave the house and nearly 2,000 acres of the estate to the National Trust. The buildings had been severely damaged by mining subsidence and considerable restoration work was needed, but the Trust has tried to make as few changes as possible, and Erddig now looks very much as it did just before the 1914–1918 War.

The estate yard, which forms the visitors' entrance to the house, is complete with large dovecote, joiners' shop, sawpit and steam-driven sawmill, blacksmith's shop and lime yard. The workshops have all been restored to operational condition. The long arched hay barn is now the National Trust's elegant shop and tearoom – it serves more substantial things than tea – and in the yard in front of it is the brick-enclosed midden in which dung from the stables was piled: the place remains, but the custom has ceased. The 18th century stable block houses carriages, early motorcars and bicycles belonging to the Yorke family and the room in the corner of the yard has an exhibition describing the restoration of Erddig by the National Trust.

The separate laundry yard was built in the 1770s and the bakehouse, scullery and wet and dry laundries were grouped around it. The very grand 18th century

The Dining Room. Erddig, Wrexham.

kitchen was originally detached from the house, but a linking block was built in the 19th century. Many of the Yorkes, incidentally, were vegetarians, which caused difficulties for the kitchen staff. The passage between the kitchen and the servants' hall contains some of the staff portraits and the remainder are in the servants' hall itself, which also contains a record of long-serving butlers, one of whom is commemorated as having died under chloroform while being operated on elsewhere in the house. The butler's pantry is impressive. The family silver, when not in use, was kept in this room, with the footman sleeping there for secur-

ity. Early 19th century suits of footmen's livery hang in one of the cupboards.

The attic bedroom and maids' work room are there for visitors to inspect and among the other rooms of particular interest are the nice little chapel and the family museum, with a delightfully old-fashioned array of human bones, a hornets' nest, old coins, swordfish blades and dozens of other treasures. Very careful attention has been paid to the restoration of the gardens. Wherever possible, the shrubs, flowers and trees that have been planted are of varieties known to have been available in the 18th and 19th centuries. Some of these have been specially propagated at Erddig, to form a collection unique in private gardens.

The North East

Worsbrough Mill Museum. *South Yorkshire County Council. Worsbrough Country Park, Worsbrough, Barnsley, South Yorkshire. The Museum is 2½ miles from the centre of Barnsley and 2½ miles from Junction 36 on the M1 motorway, along the A61 on the Barnsley-Sheffield main road. Open W.–Su. throughout the year, 10–6 in summer, 10–5 in winter.*

A mill at Worsbrough is recorded in the Domesday Survey of 1086. The present building, a water-powered corn mill, was built in about 1625. A steam-driven corn mill, with two sets of millstones, was added at the northern end of the watermill in 1843.

Worsbrough made only stone ground flour for brown bread. By the beginning of the present century, white bread, made from flour ground in large roller mills, was cheaper and more in demand, and the traditional mills fell on hard times. In 1922 the steam engine at Worsbrough was scrapped, although the water mill continued to crush barley, oats, peas and

Worsbrough Mill Museum, Barnsley, South Yorkshire.

beans for animal feed. By the 1960s, however, the machinery had become unsafe to work and the building was semi-derelict.

The milling complex then passed into the hands of the County Council, which has fully restored both mills and brought them back to operating condition, as a working museum of corn milling, where all the processes involved in producing flour from grain can be watched in action. In what is known as the New Mill, the steam engine, removed more than half a century ago, has been replaced by an oil engine built by Hornsby of Grantham in 1914. This engine, which had spent all its working life in a mill at Sykehouse, near Thorne, was rescued from the scrapyard in 1973.

Since 1976, when Worsbrough Mill was opened as a museum, a number of extra features have been added. During the month of August, the New Mill now grinds flour for sale, and a recently acquired grain-cleaning machine (c.1925) and a roller flour mill (c.1900) show 20th century changes in the milling of flour for bread. The collection of agricultural tools and equipment is being steadily enlarged and a reference collection of documents and photographs is being developed.

It is difficult to think of a better site than Worsbrough for a milling museum. A cornmill has worked continuously on the same site since at least 1625 and somewhere in the valley of the Dove – one cannot be sure of the exact site – since at least 1086. The Interpretive Centre, opposite the exit from the Old Mill, contains a display on the history and development of Worsbrough Mill, now the kind of museum which really does have something for everyone. But, should visitors happen to go away clamouring for more, their appetites whetted, the authorities have most thoughtfully provided the Worsbrough Industrial Archaeology Trail, with a special leaflet and map to explain it. There is a Short Trail and a Long Trail. The Long Trail takes two hours and includes the remains of coal mines, a horse tramway, a coal canal, a flint glassworks, a steel works, an iron foundry, a railway and a sandstone quarry.

The aim has been to make Worsbrough a museum without walls, something that a number of enterprising museums are now attempting.

Beamish: North of England Open Air Museum. *Cleveland, Durham, Northumberland, and Tyne and Wear County Councils. Beamish Hall, Beamish, Stanley, Co. Durham. Open May 1–August 31, daily 10–6. April 1–30, September 1–30, Tu.–Su. 10–6. October 1–March 31, Tu.–Su. 10–6. Open Bank Holidays.*

There is nothing quite like Beamish anywhere else in the world. Its financing and organisation is unique, a curious but efficient mixture of public and private. It is administered by a consortium of four County Councils and assisted by grants from the English Tourist Board, the Countryside Commission and other national and regional bodies, as well as by substantial contributions from industry and from the Friends of the Museum. It has been established 'to study, collect; preserve and exhibit buildings, machinery, objects and information illustrating the development of industry and the northern way of life', which is a wide enough brief for anyone. In practice, however, Beamish has decided to concentrate on the late Victorian period, which it

The interior of a terraced pit cottage. North of England Open Air Museum, Beamish.

A replica of George Stephenson's 1825 steam locomotive, Locomotion. *Beamish.*

calls 'Geordie's heyday, when the region was in the forefront of Britain's industrial development', and to do this it has created a very large and many-sided enterprise on a 200-acre estate of woodland and rolling countryside. Rural and urban history are both represented, with a reconstructed colliery and row of pit cottages; a railway system, with a complete station; a complete area of a market town; a farmworker's fully furnished cottage; the Home Farm, a restored group of farm buildings first established in 1790 and modified and added to during the 19th century.

Home Farm has three special exhibitions. One is called Harvests and Harvesting and shows how methods in the North East have changed over the years; another traces the development of various Northern breeds of farm animal; and the third deals with farm horses, with their harness and equipment. The livestock include Durham shorthorn cows and other local breeds of farm animals and poultry.

The Home Farm buildings display part of the Museum collections of agricultural machinery and hand tools. These include a horse gin dating from the 1830s, which has been rebuilt in the wheelhouse which already existed at the Home Farm; a very early type of barn thresher, dating from 1790–1800; a Mann steam tractor; and a representative collection of farm carts. There are plans to work about 100 acres of the Museum site as a mixed farm of the time of the First World War.

Beamish Hall itself has a long history.

The oldest part still standing dates from 1630, but many additions were built during the 18th and 19th centuries. It was a fashionable Victorian and Edwardian residence, with distinguished house parties. After it had been sold to meet death duties, it became the headquarters of Beamish Museum and contains, as well as the administrative offices, what is officially known as 'an A to Z selection of objects' from the huge collection.

There are frequent craft demonstrations and during the summer a number of events are organised to promote wider interest in old forms of transport. These include a Horse Driving Trial, with private driving vehicles and tradesmen's turnouts, as well as displays of heavy horses.

Colne Valley Museum. *Colne Valley Museum Trust. Cliffe Ash, Golcar, Huddersfield, West Yorkshire. Open Sa., Su. and public holidays, 2–5. Also Easter Tu. and the Tu. following Spring Bank Holiday, 2–5. Closed from the Sa. before Christmas until the Tu. after New Year's Day.*

The Museum is housed in a row of weavers' cottages, with weaving workshop on the top floor and living accommodation on the two floors below. The cottages, built c.1840, are listed buildings

Cobbler's workshop. Colne Valley Museum, Golcar.

and are in a conservation area.

The establishment of the Museum, which opened in 1970, was due entirely to local enterprise and nearly all the work of rehabilitating the cottages has been carried out by volunteers. The textile industry has a long history in the valley and the aim of the Trustees from the

beginning has been to develop a living museum, with demonstrations of 19th century life and work in authentic workshops and cottage rooms.

It is believed that Colne Valley is the only museum in Britain where hand looms can be seen working in a room originally designed and used for this purpose. Both weavers' cottages and hand looms exist elsewhere, but it is exceptional for both to be still found in the same place, particularly with the looms operating. The weavers, of course, lived on the job. They wasted no time in travelling to and from their work and they drove themselves harder than any·employer would have found it possible to do. The Museum includes a weaver's living room. The appearance of the room as it would have been in the middle of last century has

been reconstructed from pictures and written records and with the help of memories of elderly people. Most of the items in the room have been given by local families.

It has also been possible to recreate a clog-maker's workshop in one of the old weaving rooms. All the tools, furniture and equipment came from a clog-maker's premises which were set up in 1910. The Museum is reviving the craft of Yorkshire clog-making and arranges frequent demonstrations of it.

Every opportunity is given to members of school parties to live and work in the Museum rooms and, by trying their hand at the old crafts and watching the experts at work, to get a better understanding of what life was like in the Colne Valley a century ago.

Ryedale Folk Museum. *Crosland Foundation. Hutton le Hole, North Yorkshire. Open Easter–October 31, 2–5.30. July 1–August 31, also 11–2.*

The Museum, opened in 1964, is in the North Yorkshire Moors National Park. It is housed in a group of 18th century farm buildings, the curator living in the farm house and the Museum occupying the former barn, stable, cowhouse, hayloft, granary and wheelshed. The open-air section, in the grounds behind the Museum, contains a large collection of farm waggons, implements and machinery, reconstructions of houses from Danby and Harome, a fully operational smithy and the remains of an Elizabethan glass furnace.

The items displayed in the Museum are largely from Ryedale and are related to the daily lives of the people who inhabited the area from thousands of years ago to comparatively recent times. They illustrate their superstitions, their everyday tasks, their living conditions, their crafts and their pastimes.

Interior cruck house. Ryedale Folk Museum, Hutton le Hole.

In what was once the hayloft, there is a Victorian nursery scene, set up to show the toys of the period, all given by local people. The dolls' house, made in Great Barugh in about 1890, is a good representation of a Victorian interior. The adjoining room, once the granary, has more toys, including some dating from the 18th century, and a collection of washing and laundry equipment.

The main part of the barn is taken up with a representation of an important rural festival – the harvest supper. The figures at the table are dressed in early 19th century costume. Among the other exhibits in the barn is a case containing the surveying instruments of a remarkable local man, Joseph Ford, who, in the middle of the 18th century, constructed moorland watercourses to bring water to the villages on the south side of the North Yorkshire moors.

The stable shelters the working horse, Blossom, and a large array of harness, horse brasses and other trappings. Beyond the stable is the former wheelshed, with exhibits of the tools and products of many types of the country

Ryedale Folk Museum, Hutton le Hole, North Yorkshire.

craftsmen – the farrier, saddler, waggon builder, pattern maker, blacksmith, wheelwright, millstone dresser and many others. These displays are continued in a newly erected building which used 18th century roof timber, with tongued and pegged joints. A complete iron foundry, and comprehensive collections of saddlers' and joiners' tools are also to be found here.

The reconstructed buildings are all thatched. Two, from Stangend and Harome, have cruck frames – curved upright timbers resting on base stones on the ground. A second Harome cottage has the kitchen and living room furnished in typical farm fashion. The third room is set up as a dairy and has a comprehensive display of churns and butter and cheese-making equipment.

Hutton le Hole is a very agreeable village and, the Museum apart, 'we are,' says the modest Curator, 'in a part of the country which is well worth a visit anyway'.

Beck Isle Museum of Rural Life. *Beck Isle Museum Trust. Pickering, North Yorkshire. Close to Pickering Beck, off Bridge Street. Open Good Friday–July 31 and September 1–mid-October, daily 10.30–12.30, 2–5. August 1–31, 10.30–7.*

The Museum occupies a stone-built Regency house in the centre of Pickering. It is staffed and operated entirely by volunteers and was opened in 1967 to present a large collection of material reflecting the living style and rural crafts of Ryedale during the last two hundred years.

Each of the seventeen rooms has a separate theme – the Victorian Room; Domestic Equipment; Medicine, Surgery and Quackery; the Children's Room; the Costume Room – and the passages and staircases are used to display groups of miscellaneous items which cannot easily be made to attach themselves to a particular room. The Entrance Hall, for example, has two paintings of Guardsmen in a festive mood, painted by Captain Rex Whistler, as he then was, as a contribution to a children's Christmas party in 1943, when the Welsh Guards were stationed at Pickering. A small collection of military mementoes nearby includes a box of the Queen's chocolates issued to soldiers during the South African War.

In any museum of this kind, what is bound to catch one's attention is the skill, or lack of it, with which objects have been selected and combined in order to give a feeling of the past, and the way in which small items contribute to the total effect. Pickering scores well on both these counts. Every section, in total and in its individual exhibits, conveys a feeling of the essential pastness of the past, of long-vanished ways of dealing with life's practical problems. The glass-flycatchers, the net bag to hold potatoes when boiling them with a sheep's head for a stew, the pocket guinea-scales to make sure that the coins one was offered had not been clipped – all these were yesterday's ingenious answers to challenges which no longer exist.

The Museum's series of shops is one of its most popular features. The Gents Outfitters and Haberdashers is a hybrid, containing a wide variety of articles from a typical village draper's shop, together with the rather higher class stock of the outfitters in a nearby market town. The Hardware Shop recreates the crowded interior of an early twentieth century shop, stocking everything from pen-nibs to coffin plates and from gas mantles to straw hat dye. The Village Shop has the groceries and the scales to weigh them, the boiled sweets and the numbered tins, each holding a different blend of tea.

There is a good collection of farming tools, implements and vehicles, a wheelwright's shop, a blacksmith's shop and a set of cooper's tools. The legendary Moses Molley of Cropton rightly has a section to himself, with a number of the tools he used and some of his products. This remarkable craftsman is reputed to have made anything on demand, from knitting needles to washing machines. The 'knitting Nancy' and the expanding wool-winder on display are both from his workshop.

The Museum is the fortunate possessor of some excellent Victorian printing equipment, in perfect working order. On this it meets all its requirements in the way of posters, cards, leaflets and notices.

Opposite, above:
Beck Isle Museum, Pickering, North Yorkshire.
Opposite, below:
Village shop. Beck Isle Museum, Pickering.

The North West

The Museum of Bacup Natural History Society. *24 Yorkshire Street, Bacup, Lancashire. Open Th. evenings, 7.30–10, and by appointment.*

The Society and its Museum were founded in 1878. At that time, Bacup was a notoriously rough, dirty and unpleasant place. The main industry, cotton, was in a depressed condition, with only two of its 52 mills working full-time. The new Society, formed to study natural history, provided a welcome escape from the industrial misery and squalor. Its organised country rambles were particularly appreciated and attracted a wide cross-section of local people.

A museum of some kind was needed from the beginning, to house the steadily growing collection of botanical, geological and ornithological specimens discovered and presented by members. The geologists were particularly active. They always included a number of miners, whose work gave them excellent oppor-

The Museum of Bacup Natural History Society, Lancashire.

tunities to look out for fossils. During its long career, the Society has had to move its headquarters a number of times and the Museum, getting bigger all the time, has never failed to move with them. The present premises, a modest and pleasant early 19th century stone building, were formerly the Hare and Hounds public house and the Society and its Museum have been there for thirty years. An outbuilding has recently been converted into an extension of the Museum, to allow the Society to display its expanding collection of material relating to the industrial history of the area.

The Museum, like the Society, is run entirely by volunteers. Its collections of birds, insects, butterflies and flints will probably not grow a great deal more now and for some time the emphasis has been rather more on local history. The aim is to preserve a record of the town and to show how it grew to be an important cotton

manufacturing centre during the 18th and 19th centuries, how the cotton withered away, and how Bacup eventually came to make a living in other ways. To achieve this, the Museum has a wide range of photographs, domestic and industrial items, a file of the local newspaper going back to 1863 – a rich mine for the social historian – and, perhaps most valuable of all, a fine collection of records, observations and memories, set down and compiled by people who loved the town, little as it may seem to have deserved it, a long time ago.

Bacup is not yet on one of the main tourist routes and this museum is worth a visit before that sad fate happens to it. It might even be lucky enough to avoid it.

Nautical Museum, Castletown. *The Manx Museum and National Trust. Bridge Street, Castletown, Isle of Man. Open May 14–September 29, M.–Sa. 10– 1, 2–5; Su. 2–5.*

The Nautical Museum is based on the late 18th century schooner-rigged yacht, *Peggy,* and the three-storeyed boathouse

Nautical Museum, Castletown, Isle of Man.

built for her by Captain George Quayle, close to his family home, Bridge House. Above the boat cellar is a cabin room built in the form of the stern cabin of a ship of the Nelson period and designed to provide Captain Quayle and his friends with

agreeable surroundings for a convivial evening.

The 26-foot *Peggy* dates from 1791. She was mainly a pleasure boat, but she undertook some local trading. After her sailing days were over – Captain Quayle died in 1835 – she remained undisturbed in her boat cellar for a century. The archway through which she sailed into Castletown harbour was walled up and her enclosed dock was filled in. When she was rediscovered in 1935, she was immediately recognised as an exceptionally significant survival, a typical example of the small coastal craft of her day and, as such, the sort of vessel which has not normally been preserved or indeed recorded in any detail.

In 1941, *Peggy* and her boathouse were presented to the Manx Museum. The premises were restored and considerably enlarged and the Nautical Museum now installed there gives a general picture of maritime activity in the Isle of Man in the days of sail.

In Victorian times about a quarter of the population of the Island was dependent on the fishing industry for a liveli-

The Sailmaker's Loft. Nautical Museum, Isle of Man.

hood. The Museum tells the story by means of a wide range of exhibits – a fine series of models of the different types of local fishing boats; a steam-powered net-making machine, built at Douglas and operated for many years at Castletown; and an excellent collection of early photographs. Models are extensively used, too, in the section devoted to maritime trade. Both schooners and full-rigged ships are represented, two particularly interesting exhibits being those showing the Karran fleet of deep-sea vessels, registered at Castletown, and the Peel-built schooner, *Vixen*, which made a famous emigrant voyage to Australia a century ago. A connoisseur's item is a machine used at Peel for many years to manufacture ship's biscuits.

The loft of the boathouse was originally George Quayle's workshop, in which he developed his inventions. It has now been used to house a special exhibition of the techniques of sailmaking.

Clitheroe Castle Museum. *Lancashire County Museum Service. Castle Hill, Clitheroe, Lancashire. Open Easter–October 31, Tu., Th., Sa., Su., Bank Holidays, 2–4.30. July 21–August 31, daily 2–4.30*

There had to be a town at Clitheroe. Lying in a narrow belt of lowland, through which roads had to pass and with high hills on either side, it is built on and around two limestone knolls. One of them was chosen by the Normans as an impregnable site for a castle and shortly afterwards the Church of St. Mary Magdalene was built on the other. Clitheroe has been the market town of the Ribble Valley for centuries, but it has also seen considerable industrial development – cotton, synthetic fibres, quarrying.

The Norman keep, reputed to be the smallest in England, has belonged to

many families in its time, but in 1920 it was bought by the town and its 16 acres of grounds were converted into a park, one of the most sensible war memorials in the country. From the Castle there are splendid views of Clitheroe and the Ribble Valley and of the surrounding hills of Pendle and the Bowland Fells.

Built against the Castle wall at one point is an eighteenth century building, the former estate office of the Manor of

Right:
Printing display. Clitheroe Castle Museum, Lancashire.

Below:
Clitheroe Castle Museum, Lancashire.

Clitheroe. This is now the Castle Museum, with collections relating to the history, archaeology and natural history of Clitheroe and the surrounding countryside. The Museum is gradually being extended by taking over additional rooms and buildings, so that it will eventually link up with the ruined Norman keep. This will allow more room for the display of the collections of agricultural implements and waggons. For some reason, possibly the shortage of suitable museums, far fewer items of farm equipment have survived in the North-West than in other regions and those on display at Clitheroe deserve the respect due to all rarities.

Geologically, the Clitheroe area is of exceptional interest, with its famous Reef Knolls and abundance of limestone fossils. The Museum contains an important collection of local fossils, particularly the beautiful crinoids (sea lilies). Many of these have come from nearby roadstone quarries, which are very rewarding hunting grounds for the fossil enthusiast. There is no doubt that the knoll on which the Castle and the Museum stand would provide an equally rich supply, but one can reasonably assume that this particular source of limestone is safe from commercial exploitation.

Clitheroe has had a printing industry since early Victorian times and the Museum was lucky enough to acquire some of the old equipment from the town's Borough Print Works, which is displayed in the setting of a reconstructed printmaker's workshop. There are other displays on the history of printing and the craft of the bookbinder.

In a town as small as Clitheroe, there is no clear distinction to be made between the Museum and the town itself. The Museum is compact and reflects local life as a whole, showing how each part of it meshes in with the rest. Clitheroe is a museum in its own right, with its interesting mixture of old and new trades and industries, its three wells which provided the water supply until 1854, and the hooks in front of the *White Lion* which were once used for fixing hurdles to pen sheep in the Market Place. And a town which is now the administrative centre for an area containing places with such delicious names as Langho, Wilpshire, Ribchester, Grindleton and Bolton-by-Bowland could hardly be dull. Both Clitheroe and the Ribble Valley have very special personality and charm.

Cregneash Folk Museum. *Manx Museum and National Trust. Cregneash, Isle of Man. Open mid-May–September 30, M.–Sa. 10–1, 2–5; Su. 2–5.*

The Cregneash Folk Museum opened in 1938 with a single crofter's cottage. It was the first publicly owned open-air museum in the British Isles. Since then it has grown considerably and now embraces the southern end of the village, with six buildings and their adjoining gardens and walled enclosures. Other buildings and 250 acres of farm land and grazing which belonged to the people of Cregneash have also become the property of the Trust.

Cregneash is a survival of an ancient Celtic type of farming settlement. Half a dozen families worked about 300 acres of rough grazing and scattered corn-plots and formed the core of the community. Around them clustered twenty or so other families who gained a living in various

Opposite:
The Smithy. Cregneash Folk Museum, Isle of Man.

ways, such as helping the farmers, fishing, working in the leadmines and quarries, weaving, and blacksmithing.

The houses were originally one storey high and thatched. Many of the old houses at Cregneash have now been raised a storey and roofed with slate, but those belonging to the Museum are still thatched and of the traditional type. The six buildings are known as Harry Kelly's Cottage, the Turner's Shop, the Karran Farmstead, the Smithy, and the Weaver's House and Shed. Harry Kelly died in 1934. His family had lived in the village for more than 300 years and he made his livelihood with his boat and by helping local farmers. He never married and lived alone in his two-roomed cottage, which is furnished as he left it. The little group of thatched stone buildings called the Karran Farmstead belonged to a croft which farmed about 30 acres. Its old dwelling house has been used for many years as a cowhouse, after a slate-roofed house was built for the family in another part of the village.

The last hand-loom in the village is now preserved in the shed adjoining the Weaver's House. Its owner died in 1939, the last of a long line of weavers, who made the woollen cloth and flannel needed by the men of the village who went to sea, petticoats for the women, bed-covers, and carpets. They used flax and wool from the island's own breed of sheep, the Loghtan. The Trust has its own flock of Loghtan and sells knitting wool from it. The Turner's Shed contains a country joiner's treadle-lathe and his associated tools and equipment. This particular lathe was much used for making oak spinning-wheels. Cregneash had its own smithy at one time, but it stopped working before the end of last century, the the Museum's smithy is a reconstruction, with equipment gathered from various places in the Island.

One of the most difficult tasks facing the Trust has been the replacement of the thatch. The traditional Manx roped-straw thatch lasted only three years before it had to be renewed. Last century this was not a drawback, since thatchers were easy to find and charged only a shilling a day and their food. Today's labour costs, together with the scarcity of thatchers, makes it necessary to look for some other way of going about the job, although the Trust aims to keep the old tradition alive as long as it possibly can.

Dove Cottage and the Wordsworth Museum. *The Trustees of Dove Cottage. Grasmere, Ambleside, Cumbria. Open March 1–31, October 1–31, M.– Sa. 9.30–4.30. April 1–September 30, M.–Sa. 9–5.30*

Dove Cottage was the home of the poet, William Wordsworth, from 1799 to 1808. From then until 1830, the essayist and opium-eater, Thomas De Quincey, lived there. The Wordsworth Museum is near the cottage. It contains manuscripts and other material relating to the poet and a local collection which is chiefly concerned with life in the Grasmere district in Wordsworth's time. The collections have been greatly enhanced recently by the purchase of manuscripts of poems and letters by members of the Wordsworth circle, and also by several important loans, including paintings, prints and drawings from the National Portrait Gallery and the Victoria and Albert Museum.

A major restructuring of the exhibition should be completed by 1981, with the opening of the Wordsworth Heritage Centre, to be housed in a large converted

Coachhouse/barn next to Wordsworth's Dove Cottage, Grasmere.

barn and coachhouse next to the cottage. The present Museum will then be converted into a library.

Dove Cottage was built as an inn, called the Dove and Olive Bough, in the early 17th century. It had six rooms and the eight years of 'plain living and high thinking' that Wordsworth spent there, first with his sister and then with his wife as well, were among the happiest of his life. Most of the furniture now here belonged to the Wordsworths. It came into the possession of the Trustees gradually, after the cottage had been bought for the nation in 1890. The decorations are much as they were in 1808.

The Wordsworths stocked the garden with ferns, wild flowers and mosses brought back from their walks, and with plants given to them by neighbours. They planted shrubs and apple trees and grew runner beans up the wall of the house. Care has been taken to keep the garden as nearly as possible as it was when the Wordsworths looked after it, but their vegetable plot is now a little lawn.

With a growing family, the house eventually became too small. After two very local moves, the Wordsworths went to Rydal Mount, close by, in 1813 and stayed there for the rest of their lives. De Quincey's tenancy came to an end in 1836 and from then until 1890 the cottage had a succession of tenants, some of them local people.

The Wordsworth Museum was constructed during the 1930s from the old barn adjoining Sykeside, home of Molly Fisher, the Wordsworths' servant. The ground floor contains exhibits illustrating the life of the neighbourhood in the 18th and 19th centuries. The upper floor is devoted to the Wordsworths and the members of their circle. There are manuscripts of the poems and of Dorothy

Wordsworth's *Journals*, portraits of the poet by various artists, the Wordsworth family Bible, and a Prayer Book giving the dates of births and deaths in the family. There are also a number of the poet's personal possessions. They include two fancy waistcoats and the shade he wore to protect his eyes from the glare of candles.

Hawkshead Courthouse. *The National Trust. Hawkshead, Cumbria. At junction of Ambleside and Coniston roads, half a mile north of Hawkshead on B5286. Open Easter weekend, then May 1–October 30, daily except M., including Bank Holiday M., 2–5.*

The Courthouse came into the possession of the National Trust in 1932. It is now a branch of the Museum of Lakeland Life and Industry at Kendal (q.v.), an interesting little museum in a very agreeable part of the country.

In the 12th century the manor of Hawkshead became part of the lands of the Abbey of Furness. The Abbey obtained important revenue from the sheep

Hawkshead Courthouse, Cumbria.

farms, coppice woods, forges and bloomeries, to which the iron from Low Furness was brought for smelting. To administer the property, the monks set up a headquarters at Hawkshead Hall, which they built for the purpose. All that is left of this today is the Courthouse. This has an arched entrance passing through it, rooms at ground level which originally served as porters' lodges and a large room above where the manor courts were probably held.

After the Dissolution of the Monasteries the Manor of Hawkshead had many owners and the Courthouse has had a variety of uses. In its present form as a museum, it contains tools, implements and artifacts reflecting the cultural and industrial life of the Lakeland fells, from medieval times to the recent past. The exhibits are grouped in seven Bays, called Place, The Nursery, Hearth and Home The Farm, The Woollen Industry, The Woodland Industries, and Iron. This makes it possible to present a good range of characteristic Lakeland exhibits within a small space, without allowing the Museum to become a mere hotchpotch. Until this century, the Cumbrian dales were very isolated and ancient traditions and old farming practices died hard. Some of the implements on show were peculiar to the area and others continued in use in this part of Britain long after they had been given up elsewhere. The breastplough, for example, pushed by the operator's chest or thighs, was still used in Cumbria in the 19th century and corn was threshed with the flail even within living memory.

The Herdwich sheep, the traditional local breed, produce a coarse fleece, which gives the woollen cloth produced in the Lake District its characteristic look and feel. The Museum has examples of both fleeces and cloth, including a piece woven at Troutbeck in the eighteenth century, with the red, yellow and black colours produced by vegetable dyes. John Peel's 'coat so grey' was made from an undyed material, woven from a mixture of the wool of white, black and brown sheep. Most of the Dale dwellers, men and women, were engaged in knitting hosiery as well as in spinning and weaving and the Museum has examples of their hand-carved knitting sticks. To make stockings last longer, the feet were smeared with pitch and then dragged through the ashes of a peat fire, forming a hard, flexible sole which stood up well to wear.

Hodbarrow, in south Cumbria, had the richest deposits of haematite, the red iron ore, in Britain during the 18th and 19th centuries and the Museum has relics of this once important industry, including miners' clogs stained red by the ore. The Lakeland dales were involved in ironworking in a different way. Charcoal made from wood in their coppices was used to smelt the ore brought up from the bell pits of Low Furness. The Museum has examples of the type of iron produced in this way until the 1920s. Charcoal burning continued longer, since it was used in another local industry, the manufacture of gunpowder. The last gunpowder works closed in 1937.

Higher Mill Museum, Helmshore. *Lancashire County Council. Holcombe Road, Helmshore, Rossendale, Lancashire. Open M.–Sa., 2–5, including Bank Holidays.*

This 18th century water-powered fulling mill, now scheduled as an Historic

Monument, lies in the valley of the River Ogden in the Rossendale 'Forest' area of

Lancashire. Carefully and sympathetically restored, it illustrates an important stage in the development of the textile industry from its rural origins.

Fulling is the beating or, earlier, treading process which causes the fibres in woollen cloth to mat and interlock. It produces a heavy dense fabric suitable for such products as blankets and overcoats. Higher Mill, which was operating by the early 1790s, was one of the first mills to be erected in Rossendale. Previously, weavers had to make use of the Rochdale fulling mills and to transport their cloth by packhorse.

Originally Higher Mill had two relatively narrow waterwheels. The arches of their wheelpits can still be seen. They were replaced by the present large wheel in the middle of the 19th century. The

Higher Mill Museum, Helmshore.

gearing broke down in 1954 and this put an end to the commercial operation of the mill. The waterwheel, which by the 1970s was in a decrepit condition, has now been thoroughly restored.

The first fulling machines, or fulling stocks, were very solid, noisy affairs. They consisted of heavy wooden hammers which pounded the wet cloth at between 30 and 40 beats a minute. This type of machine can be seen at Helmshore. It took a whole working day to full a 30-yard

Opposite, above:
Burns' Cottage, Alloway, Strathclyde.
Opposite, below:
Carlyle's Birthplace, Ecclefechan, Dumfries and Galloway.

piece of cloth. Rotary machines, also represented in the Museum, were introduced in the 1840s and did the job much faster. The length of cloth was sewn into an endless loop and rotated continuously through the machine, pressure being applied by the spring-loaded milling roller.

Other machinery and equipment on show at Helmshore includes a tub on wheels, which was taken from house to house to collect urine, in which the cloth was steeped or lacked before fulling. This removed the lanolin or grease from the cloth. In the early 19th century a more convenient form of ammoniacal liquor became available from gasworks. The exhibit at Helmshore is a rare survival

from a more primitive age.

Immediately before fulling, the cloth was soaked in a soap, soda ash or acid solution which was the milling agent. This had to be rinsed away after fulling and the fulled cloth was then put through a mangle to squeeze the water out, tentered – stretched and straightened as it dried – and passed over teazle-covered rollers to raise the nap. Helmshore has examples of all this equipment, together with an internationally famous collection of early machinery for preparing and spinning cotton. This includes original Arkwright machinery, installed in about 1790 in his mills at Cromford, in Derbyshire.

Helmshore is well worth a special journey.

Abbot Hall Art Gallery and Museum of Lakeland Life and Industry.
Lake District Art Gallery Trust. Kendal, Cumbria. On A6 south of town centre and adjoining Parish Church. M.–F. 10.30–5.30; Sa., Su. 2–5 (Art Gallery). M.–F. 10.30–12.30, 2–5; Sa., Su. 2–5 (Museum). Closed Good Friday and 2 weeks over Christmas and New Year.

Abbot Hall was built in 1759 on the site of an earlier house. It was bought, very cheaply, by Kendal Corporation in 1897. The grounds became a public park but the house remained virtually uninhabited for half a century. After extensive renovation it was opened to the public in 1962. The ground floor was restored to its original 18th century splendour and the upper storey converted into modern galleries with top lighting. The furnishings are to a large extent of local origin, including items by Gillows of Lancaster.

Opposite, above:
The Musicians' Gallery and Assembly Hall of Hamilton District Museum, Strathclyde.
Opposite, below:
Bella Pol's House. Auchindrain Museum of Country Life, Inveraray, Strathclyde.

The 18th century stable block later became the Museum of Lakeland Life and Industry. It has since acquired additional accommodation in the adjoining 16th century Grammar School. The Museum illustrates the life and means of livelihood of Lakeland people, past and present, against a background of the hills which have conditioned a tough and resilient people. There are exhibits relating to mining, quarrying – especially of the Lake District's beautiful slate – sheep and dairy farming and a wide range of rural industries dependent on the water power with which the Lake District is so generously provided – weaving and fulling, bobbin-making, the manufacture of gunpowder and brushes.

There is a reproduction of a Lakeland farm parlour, as it was in the early years of the present century, when living con-

ditions had become a good deal more comfortable than they had been fifty years earlier. Other exhibits deal with laundering – most Lakeland water is very soft and a welcome saver of soap – cooking, ablutions, clothing, and travelling equipment. There is also a collection of Arthur Ransome's possessions, including his desk and chair and his chess set.

The south wing of the former stable block houses relics of farming, old industries and rural trades. The region was to a large extent isolated from the rest of Britain in the past and this compelled its blacksmiths and engineers to become inventive and enterprising. Many of Lakeland's modern factories have grown up from the little village workshops established in Victorian times and earlier. The Museum has an exceptionally fine collection of local craftsmen's tools and machines. One of the most interesting displays is of the making of mill bobbins for the Lancashire cotton industry. There were plentiful supplies of coppice wood available for the purpose and bobbin mills were to be found along most convenient streams. The floors were always covered with piles of shavings, which is no doubt the reason why so many of the mills were burnt down.

In both the craft and farming sections, the Museum takes the visitor through to the introduction of mechanisation. It has the first water turbine, made by Williamsons of Kendal, a very early steam clothing press, by Messrs. Isaac Braithwaite, an early barn threshing machine driven by an oil engine and a large automatic bobbin turning lathe, built by Braithwaites in 1881 and in continuous use until recently.

One of the most remarkable examples of Lakeland inventiveness shown at Abbot Hall is an earth closet operated by an ingenious lever system that riddled a charge of sand down into the receptacle when a person's weight was lifted from the seat.

Both the Art Gallery and the Museum have constantly changing exhibitions, covering a very wide range of subjects, which avoids the frustration, both for visitors and for the Museum staff, of having a large part of the collections perpetually buried away out of sight.

Croxteth Country Park. *Merseyside County Museums. Croxteth Hall Lane, Liverpool, Merseyside. On the A5049, at the junction of Muirhead Avenue East and Oak Lane. Walled Garden: open June 1–September 16, daily ex. M., 1–6. Country Park: daily 9–dusk.*

Croxteth, officially subtitled 'Living Countryside in a City', deserves an entry in the *Guide* for sheer imagination and courage. The 530-acre estate, once the family seat of the Earls of Sefton, was given to Merseyside County Council after the death of the 7th Earl in 1972. It was then decided to use part of the estate for

Opposite:
The Wheelwright's Shop. Museum of Lakeland Life and Industry, Kendal.

the development of a commercial and educational farm and to demonstrate horticultural techniques in the walled garden. A woodland reserve is being established and all the features that help to create a rural atmosphere will be maintained or improved. In the formal gardens there are several acres of freshwater, the largest of which were originally created as ornamental pools, well-stocked with fish, including trout. Within the woodland, numerous marlpits have filled

with water. These pits have a variety of
wildlife and some of them are now available
for fishing.

More than a hundred species of birds
have been observed in the park and sixty
of them are known to have bred there in
recent years. Of the rest, about twenty
occur as winter visitors and twenty as
migrants which stay for only a few days or
hours.

The Walled Garden was built early in
the 19th century and illustrates the lavish
expenditure which was typical of large
private estates in Victorian and Edwardian times. It covers two acres and was
planned and operated to provide the
house with fruit, vegetables, cut flowers
and pot plants throughout the year. The
thirty gardeners employed there had to
look after no fewer than twenty-four glass-

Aerial view of Croxteth Country Park, Liverpool.

houses, growing grapes, pineapples, melons, cucumber, cherries, plums and peaches, as well as the usual outdoor fruits and vegetables. Imported fruits were difficult to obtain and great establishments like Croxteth had the pleasant habit of bringing pot-grown fruit trees to the table, so that guests could pick oranges or cherries as part of the dessert course.

As far as possible, the Museum reproduces the original crops and conditions in the Walled Garden, to show how Victorian gardeners carried out their extremely skilled tasks. Beekeeping, too, is practised here, as it always was, with the bees benefitting from the same sheltered climate as the fruits and flowers.

Building of the Hall began in 1575 and there were several major additions before the west wing was completed in 1902. It grew in size as the Seftons grew in wealth and importance. A range of rooms on the first floor has been furnished to illustrate the lifestyle of this noble and powerful family as it was in Edwardian times. The formal gardens were laid out and planted

over the same long period, and resulted in the introduction of many exotic trees and shrubs.

Croxteth offers a rare, if not unique opportunity for the city dweller to learn something of the countryside, and of a country estate designed to fit the sporting interests of its owners. To be able to see farming, forestry and game management in action only five miles from the centre of Liverpool is no small achievement.

'The Grove' Rural Life Museum. *The Manx Museum and National Trust. Andreas Road, Ramsey, Isle of Man. Open mid-May–September 30, M.–F. 10–5; Su. 2–5.*

The innovations in transport, in farming, in commerce and in technology, which brought so many changes in the pattern and style of life in the Isle of Man in the 19th century are shown here in relation to the home of a businessman of that period. This is how he lived and this is what was happening around him. 'The Grove' is a small, pleasant early Victorian house. It

was built for a family of some social standing in the district, at a time when a middle-class household was still to a large extent self-contained, with servants available to carry out the wide range of tasks

Drawing Room of 'The Grove' Rural Life Museum. Ramsey, Isle of Man.

which had to be performed on the premises.

This is a new museum, opened in 1978, and it has been planned in an interesting way. The idea, broadly speaking, has been to say, 'This was a fairly well-to-do middle-class home. Only the shell, the house, is left, but, if we fill it with the kind of things these people and their neighbours would have used, we shall be able to communicate something of the quality of their lives, a mixture of country and town which no longer exists?'

So in the house there are the period rooms, kitchen, drawing room, dining room and sewing room, the Victorian shower bath, and the Garden room, with its range of early beekeeping equipment. Moving from room to room one notices such pleasant attentions to detail as the Broadwood piano of 1836 and Victorian music, the period greeting cards, the fern-decorated sewing table, the Victorian wallpaper and the well-scrubbed kitchen table and dresser.

In the outbuildings is that symbol of respectability, the phaeton, and a number of exhibits to remind us of the still-rural society to which Ramsey belonged at that time – a horse-driven threshing mill, farm vehicles and an exhibition of agricultural equipment. As one passes into the grounds, there is an introductory display, putting the house in its historical and geographical setting, and then the duck pond, the fish pond and a small flock of the traditional Manx breed of Loghtan sheep. The garden has been restored as far as possible to its Victorian appearance, allowing for the fact that most of the trees are a good deal bigger than anything that was there in the 1840s. Restoration has its limits.

Thornton Windmill. *Lancashire County Museum Service. Marsh Mill, Thornton Cleveleys, Lancashire. Open June 1–August 31, Su. 2–6; W. 6–9.*

Marsh Mill was built in 1794. It is probably the finest surviving example in Britain of an 18th century windmill built for grinding corn and the only complete windmill of any period in the North-West. The original wooden shafts and gearing are still in place, driving four pairs of six-foot millstones. For the first hundred years of its life it produced flour, but at the turn of the century, when the new sophisticated machinery, driven first by steam and later by electricity, was creating a demand for a finer, white flour, Marsh Mill went over to grinding animal feeding stuffs. After being used for some years as a café it passed into the possession of Thornton Urban District Council and is now administered by the County Museums Service. During the past ten years, it has been carefully restored, with the help of voluntary workers. There is an active Thornton Windmill Preservation Society.

It is a big mill – the top floor is 70 feet above the ground – and visitors are taken over it on leisurely-paced tours which provide ample opportunity to study the details of the machinery, with its complicated and massive gearing, and to observe how the different processes gradually move the grain from the top to the bottom of the mill. The sails, 30 feet long, are of the type the Mill carried when it was first built at the end of the 18th century. With these sails, Marsh Mill had up to 60 horsepower, with, of course, no expenditure whatever on fuel.

Very large timbers were involved in building and equipping the Mill, which had to withstand great wind pressure, as

well as the vibration and weight of the machinery. The main framework of the cap is formed by two sheer beams, more than a foot in section, which are connected by a number of almost equally substantial crossbeams. The vertical shaft, which takes the power down from the cap to the stones is a solid piece of oak two feet in diameter. An exceptionally magnificent tree would have been required to produce a timber of this size.

Each pair of stones weighed about two tons when new. The upper stones rotated at about 125 revolutions a minute – the lower stones were fixed – and at least ten horsepower was needed to drive one stone, so that Marsh Mill's 60 horsepower was none too much. As the stones wore down in use, the furrows in them had to be recut, and in a busy mill like the one at Thornton this was necessary about once a month. The balance of the wheels and the distance between them was also critical, to avoid excessive friction and to make sure that the right texture of meal was obtained.

Nowhere in Britain is it possible to obtain a better idea of the skill involved in building, maintaining and operating the wonderfully efficient complex of machinery which a windmill was, a mechanical laboratory and training ground where many of the best engineers of the 18th and 19th centuries learnt their craft and developed their inventions. It was also, apart from the blacksmith's, the most important centre of the rural economy in areas where the local streams and rivers were inadequate to power watermills. Mills like Marsh Mill were, in a very real sense, the power houses of much of the English countryside.

Opposite:
Marsh Mill, Thornton Cleveleys,
Lancashire.

Scotland

Burns' Cottage. *Trustees of Burns' Monument. Alloway, Ayr. Near junction of Alloway main street and Doonholm road. April 1–September 30, M.–Sa. 9–7. June 1–August 31, also Su. 10–7. April 1–May 31 and September 1–30, Su. 2–7. Earlier closing in winter. Closed winter Sundays, December 25, 26, and January 1, 2.*

In 1756, while he was working as a gardener for Provost William Fergusson, at his estate of Doonholm, William Burnes – he spelt his name with an e, but his children, for some reason, dropped it – took a lease on 7½ acres of land at Alloway, with the intention of setting up as a market-gardener and nurseryman. He built a cob house with his own hands – the 'auld clay biggin' – went to live there in 1757 with his bride, Agnes Broun. Their eldest son, the poet Robert Burns, was born there in 1759. In 1766 the family moved to Mount Oliphant, two miles away, where William Burnes began farming on a small scale. The cottage at Alloway was let for some years to various tenants and then, in 1781, it was sold to the Incorporation of Shoemakers of Ayr, who turned it into an alehouse.

A century later, in 1881, the property was bought by the Alloway Burns Monument Trustees, who had erected the Monument, close by on the banks of the Doon, in 1820-23. When they came into possession of the cottage, they set about restoring it to its original condition and converting it into a Burns museum. The Monument and the Cottage, 600 yards away, now form a single property, linked and surrounded by pleasant, well cared for gardens. Together, they contain what the Trustees described as 'the largest collection of Burnsiana in the world', which is another way of saying that they have acquired and put on show a remarkable range and number of mementoes of the poet, his family and his friends.

These include numerous pieces of furniture – the chair in which Mrs. William Burnes nursed her children; a bannock

Burns' Cottage. Alloway.

toaster given to Robert Burns' wife, Jean Armour, as a wedding present; a mahogany chest of drawers and writing desk, which belonged to the poet himself – and an impressive variety of Burns' own possessions, the family Bible which he bought new for £2 in 1788 and which cost the Trustees £1,700 in 1904; a pair of pistols carried by Burns when he was an Exciseman; six of his waistcoat buttons; an inkwell in a leather case, with two quills and a knife for trimming them; his razor and shaving mirror. There is also a plaster cast of his skull and, of course, a lock of his hair.

The museum is richly endowed with manuscripts and early editions of the poems – the manuscript of 'Auld Lang Syne', the proof sheet of 'Tam O'

Shanter', the little four-page quarto of 'Holy Willie's Prayer', a presentation copy from Robert Burns to Miss Graham of Fintry of the 1793 volume. 'A Selection Collection of Original Scottish Airs for the Voice', and dozens of others. There are, as well, family documents of all kinds – letters to friends, agreements with publishers, a communication to Burns' sister, saying she is to receive a State pension of £20, a journal of a tour in the Highlands which Burns made in 1787, to Miss McMurdo of Drumlanrig, 'inclosing a

song composed on her'. And there are many portraits and drawings.

In the course of time, the Museum has generated its own antiquities. On the walls of the East Room, for instance, one can see two mementoes of Royal visits, leaves from the Visitor Books, bearing the signatures of the Prince of Wales, who came to the Cottage in 1926, and of Queen Elizabeth and Prince Philip, who were there thirty years later. Few small museums have been so fortunate.

Scottish Fisheries Museum. *Scottish Fisheries Museum Trust. St. Ayles, Harbourhead, Anstruther, Fife. Open April–October, M.–Sa., 10–12.30 and 2.30–6; Su. 2–5; November–March, W.–M. 2.30–4.30.*

Unbelievable as it may sound, this is the only museum in the British Isles which is devoted entirely to the fishing industry and the people who work in it. Opened in 1969 and subsequently considerably extended, it is housed in a group of

buildings known as St. Ayles, at the Scottish fishing port of Anstruther. St.

Model of a c. 1900 Scottish East Coast fisherman's home. Scottish Fisheries Museum, Anstruther.

Ayles has recorded connections with fishing which go back to 1318. Among the buildings which now form part of the Museum are the 16th century Abbot's Lodging, where the Abbot of Balmerino and his officers used to stay during their visits to Anstruther, and a house built by the brewer, William Lumsden, in 1821 and later used as a ship's chandler's shop. For the restoration and conversion work carried out on these two buildings, the Trust received an Architectural Heritage Year Award in 1975.

The Museum includes four broad categories of material – fish, fishing people, ships and equipment. The fish and shellfish to be found in Scottish waters can be seen swimming about live in the Marine Aquarium and the Floor Pool, but the fishing people, alas, are all presented in the form of models and paintings, especially those by John McGhie. There are many exhibits, however, to illustrate their activities, past and present. The living room of a fisher family and a fisherman's net loft, both of about 1900, have been reconstructed, with authentic contents, and elsewhere there are exhibits illustrating the ancillary trades, such as sack-making and coopering and collections of personal items belonging to fishermen.

One complete gallery is given up to explaining the different methods of catching fish, with dioramas, model fishing boats and examples of fishing gear. There is a whaling exhibition, which contains, among other interesting items, logs of voyages made in 1830 and 1834 by a whaling skipper from Cellardyke. A large map of the North Atlantic fishing grounds has been painted, very effectively, straight on to the stone wall at the end of the main exhibition gallery. This hall displays the major collection of model fishing vessels, a selection of navigation instruments and ship's gear, and a walk-through wheelhouse, complete with working radio and radar.

Not all the exhibits are indoors. In the cobbled courtyard near the entrance gatehouse is a large anchor, weighing about a ton, which was picked up in the net of a local fishing boat, and behind it is a strange structure of wooden spars, known as Gallowses, a relic of the days when fishermen 'barked' their nets, by steeping them in tanks of boiling water and oak bark, to preserve the cotton against the action of the sea-water, and then hung them over the gallowses to dry.

Pride of place among the outdoor exhibits must, however, go to the 70-foot fishing boat, *Fifie*, which has been restored and is now able to move and, if need be, fish, under her own sail.

Hugh Miller's Cottage. *The National Trust for Scotland. Highland Church Street, Cromarty, Highland. Open May 1–September 30, M.–Sa. 10–12, 1–5. June 1–September 30, also Su. 2–5.*

This is the cottage in which the stone-mason-poet, Hugh Miller, was born in 1802. It has been open to the public as a museum since 1900. Built in 1711 by Miller's great-grandfather, John Fiddes, it is now the last remaining thatched cottage in Cromarty and gives a good idea of what the old Fishertown houses must have looked like before slates replaced rushes for roofing.

Miller was seventeen when he decided to become a stonemason and he worked at the craft for fifteen years, travelling over the north of Scotland and the Lothians in the course of his work. During his wandering years as an apprentice and

journeyman mason he became very interested in geology and collected folklore
and legends, all of which knowledge he
turned to account later in his writings.
The hard life of a journeyman under-
mined his health and his later years as a
craftsman were spent at Cromarty, where
he was able to live at home and work on

*Hugh Miller's Cottage, Cromarty,
Highland.*

smaller jobs, such as tombstones and
sundials.

When he was thirty-two, he married
and deserted the workbench for an office
stool, joining the Commercial Bank of

Scotland as accountant at their newly-opened Cromarty branch. Meanwhile, he was writing a great deal, especially on religious matters. He was closely involved in religious controversy and in 1840 went to Edinburgh as editor of the Evangelical Party's new newspaper, *The Witness*. He became a well-known and picturesque figure in Edinburgh. After sixteen years at the centre of religious and political argument, the strain became too much for him and he shot himself on Christmas Eve, 1856.

The Museum at Cromarty reflects the different aspects of his career. The room, 'half buried in the eaves', in which he was born is devoted to his boyhood and to his days as a stonemason. Across the landing from here is a room commemorating his achievements as a writer. It contains manuscripts and early editions of his works, geological drawings and a number of letters to him on various subjects from Darwin, Carlyle and other great men of the day. Also in this room is the high desk at which he worked in the Commercial Bank from 1835 to 1840 and, as a symbol of his last years, a file of *The Witness*. The Geology Room combines an exhibition of rocks and fossils from the areas best known to Miller with a selection of his writings on geological subjects.

In the little garden there is a sundial made by Hugh Miller himself during his convalescence in 1834. He was very proud of it, believing it showed 'that my skill as a stone cutter rises somewhat above the average of the profession'. And from the garden one can see the column carrying the statue which was erected by public subscription to one of the most remarkable self-taught men of the century.

Preston Mill and Phantassie Doocot. *The National Trust for Scotland. Off the A1, 5½ miles west of Dunbar, East Lothian. Open April 1–September 30, M.–Sa. 10–12.30, 2–7.30; Su. 2–7.30. October 1–March 31, closes at 4.30.*

Grain has been milled on this site since the 12th century and much of the existing fabric dates from the 17th. The mill was extensively renovated in 1760 and the iron waterwheel, 13 feet in diameter and just over 3 feet wide, was cast in that year, probably at the Carron foundry at Falkirk. Except for one brief interval, for reasons described below, the mill has been in continuous operation ever since and visitors can see how it has always worked, from the drying of the grain in the kiln, with its picturesque pantile-covered roof, to the production of the oatmeal from the millstones, ready for bagging.

In 1948 the old mill somehow survived one of the greatest floods in its history. The River Tyne rose as high as the eaves of the building. Volunteer effort succeeded in carrying out a nearly complete

Phantassie Doocot, Dunbar, Lothian.

Preston Water Mill. East Lothian.

restoration, but by the Sixties it had become clear that some form of permanent subsidy was needed if Preston Mill was to be maintained as a working mill. In 1966 salvation appeared in the form of Rank Hovis McDougall, who decided to adopt the mill. They put the machinery into first-class order and, by providing the necessary money and moral support, made it possible for experienced millers to act as custodians of the mill when they reached the age of retirement and in this way to keep the wheels and the stones turning.

Phantassie Doocot, the Mill's near neighbour, was given to the Trust in 1961. It is one of the biggest and most remarkable dovecotes in the British Isles. Built of solid masonry, four feet thick at the base, it has nesting places for 500 birds. The walls project upwards in the form of a horseshoe-shaped hood, to enclose a sloping tiled roof. This faces south, so that the doves could have the maximum benefit of sunshine and shelter.

Carlyle's Birthplace. *The National Trust for Scotland. Ecclefechan, Dumfries and Galloway. Just of A74, 9 miles north-west of Gretna Green. Open April 4– October 31, M.–Sa. 10–6.*

The writer, Thomas Carlyle, was born in 1795 in this archway house in the main street of Ecclefechan. The house was built by his father and uncle, both of whom were master masons.

The room in which Carlyle was born is furnished not as a bedroom, but as a writer's workroom. It contains a number of his personal belongings and an important series of his letters. The adjoining bedroom has his cradle and a box bed. The kitchen, on the ground floor, is furnished and equipped in a way which would have seemed familiar to Carlyle's parents.

It was from here that Thomas Carlyle, at the age of eleven, was taken by his father to Annan Academy. He was, according to his mother, 'a lang, sprawling, ill-put-together thing'.

Thomas Carlyle's Birthplace (b. 1795). Ecclefechan.

The West Highland Museum. *West Highland Museum Trust. Cameron Square, Fort William, Highland. Open mid-September–mid-June, M.–Sa. 9.30–1, 2–5. Mid-June–mid-September, M.–Sa. 9.30–9.*

This independent museum celebrated its fiftieth anniversary in 1972. After a few years in temporary premises, the steadily growing collections were moved to the present building, formerly a bank, in 1925. The aim has been to record, preserve and display items of historical significance within the West Highland area. The contents range from Stone Age artifacts to modern industry, with a special emphasis on the Jacobite risings of the 18th century.

There are six exhibition rooms. Room One is concerned with military matters, with the Church, with coinage and with whisky distilling, a curious but attractive combination which communicates very well the essence of the history of the Highlands. Room Two deals with natural history and the weather and with a number of important economic developments, such as the building of the West Highland Railway, the coming of electricity and the beginnings of the aluminium and paper industries. Room Three is devoted to the rough and bloody history of Fort William. Room Four is mainly geological and archaeological, but also includes exhibitions relating to crofting and to the building of the Caledonian Canal, an immensely costly project which never brought the benefits intended from it. Planned to prevent sailing ships from the delays and danger of the route round the north of Scotland, it was made unnecessary by the arrival of steamships. Room Five is the House of Stewart – Stuart was the French spelling – and Bonnie Prince Charlie, 'a sour, disappointed man, often drunk and violent in temper'. The very choice collections in Room Five include the Secret Portrait of the Prince. The panel appears to be only a meaningless

The 'Secret Portrait' of Bonnie Prince Charlie, The West Highland Museum, Fort William, Highland.

pattern of paint, but when used as a tray, a perfect likeness is reflected in a glass standing on it.

The whole of Room Six is for dress and the clans. A number of myths and misconceptions are blown away in these two rooms. Many tartans, reputedly traditional, are, it appears, of quite recent design and old prints and portraits often show individuals wearing a variety of setts – repeating chequered designs – in different articles of clothing. The kilt, the Museum patiently and attractively explains, dates only from the late 18th century. Before that, men dressed in a shirt and a very long untailored piece of cloth called a plaid. Putting on the plaid was quite a business and most visitors are likely to be fascinated by the instructions as to how to go about it. To dress, the Highlander put his shirt on and then laid the plaid on the ground in rough pleats on top of his belt. He then lay down on it, fastened the belt round his waist and got to his feet, arranging the folds as he did so and draping the spare cloth round his shoulders, where a large round brooch held it in place. A Highlander could not dress standing up, and the pilgrimage to the West Highland Museum is well worthwhile, if only to discover that.

Angus Folk Museum. *The National Trust for Scotland. Kirk Wynd, Glamis, Tayside. Open May 1–September 30, daily 1–6, and on request.*

The Angus Folk Collection was made by Jean, Lady Maitland, and was formerly the property of local trustees. It was given to the National Trust for Scotland in 1974 and is housed in Kirkwynd Cottages, a row of six 17th century stone-roofed cottages, presented to the Trust by the late Earl of Strathmore and subsequently restored.

Lady Maitland made her collection over a period of forty years. She began it after meeting Isabel Grant, the founder of the Highland Folk Museum at Kingussie. For some years, the material was kept and arranged in six rooms of the Manse at Rescobie. In 1953, it was opened as a museum at Rescobie and four years later it was transferred to Glamis, where it still is.

The collection illustrates every aspect of country life in the past. It is arranged in sections – a Domestic Section, Church Relics and Agricultural Section, Tradesmen's Tools, Old Cottage Industries, Lighting in Olden Times, Old Madge's Kitchen, Weapons and Firearms, Tobacco and Snuff, the Manse Parlour, Music. To visitors from south of the border, many of the names of the objects

Kirkwynd Cottages. Angus Folk Museum, Glamis, Tayside.

Angus Folk Museum. Glamis.

will appear strange and sometimes incomprehensible. Luggies, plump churns, heughs, salmon leisters, quaichs, flauchter spades, thraw-crooks, and creepie-chairs are a foreign language, although once one sees the article in question the meaning is usually clear enough.

Some of the exhibits certainly need their explanatory caption, though, like the big wooden bowl with an iron ball in it for grinding mustard, and the 'mealie student's scoop' – poor students took a sack of meal and a barrel of salt herrings back to the university with them in order to sustain themselves during the term. And the wooden chalice must have been rare outside Angus.

Lady Maitland always felt it rather out of place to have farm implements inside the cottages. 'No Angus housewife,' she

pointed out, 'would have allowed these inside her door.' So eventually a new agricultural annexe was built across the road and the cottages were cleansed of the ploughs, thatching tools and turnip cutters. The showpiece in this section is the workbench and lathe belonging to the Rev. Patrick Bell, minister of Carmyllie and inventor of the reaping machine, but, among the more mundane potato-diggers, saddles and pumps there are a number of smaller articles which show the inventiveness and craftsmanship of our ancestors – a hot-water bottle adapted for feeding piglets, leather boots to help horses stand up on icy roads and a blackberry-comb, for speeding up the gathering of these small wild berries.

Glencoe and North Lorn Folk Museum. *Folk Museum Trust. Glencoe Village, Highland. Open May 1–September 30, M.–Sa. 10–5.30.*

In this particular place, the temptation for a museum to become obsessed with the Massacre of Glencoe is very great, especially with so many of the annual crop of 30,000 and more visitors coming from England and overseas. Perhaps the greatest tribute one can pay the Museum is to say that such a temptation has been successfully resisted. The Massacre is present in the Museum, but it is not omnipresent.

The Museum is very much a piece of local enterprise. Established in 1967, it moved in 1972 to its present home, a cruck cottage in the centre of the village. It has the traditional heather thatch, the only house in the village still roofed in this way, and much more accommodation has since been made available as a result of the restoration of outbuildings behind the cottage, which were in a derelict condition when the Museum took them over. These, too, have been thatched with heather and now contain the Dairying exhibits.

Slate quarrying was for a long time an important industry in the Glencoe area. At the present time, the derelict area around the quarry is being cleaned up and landscaped, removing most of the evidence of how it all looked in its working days. The Museum, however, has preserved a number of tools and other relics of the industry, so that what was a major source of local employment shall not be wholly forgotten. These exhibits are supported by a collection of photographs, postcards and printed matter which illustrate living and working conditions in and around Glencoe from Victorian times onwards.

The objects in the Museum are mainly concerned with the home and with farming. In the past, existence in Glencoe has been far from gentle, with work hard to find and amenities of a minimal nature. This little Museum presents, in a modest and homely way, the way in which life has gradually changed in the district, especially during the past 50 years.

It would have been unfair and ungracious of the Museum to ignore military matters altogether and visitors are given a very reasonable ration – 18th century rampart guns from Glengarry Castle, a selection of smaller guns and swords, some Jacobite items and a number of relics of the Chiefs of Glencoe. And it is always possible, of course, to sally forth into the Pass of Glencoe and reconstruct the bloody scene for oneself, if one's inclinations should happen to lead in that direction.

Hamilton District Museum. *Hamilton District Council. 129 Muir Street, Hamilton, Strathclyde. Open M.–F., 10–12, 1–5; Sa. 10–5.*

The main section of the Museum building dates from the 17th century. It was formerly an inn, the Hamilton Arms. Coaches to and from London used to halt here and in 1790 extensive stables were built to accommodate the horses. Part of the stable block survives and forms part of the Museum. Adjoining the stable is a newly-built wing, used to house the Museum's large transport collection, and in what was once the inn the Assembly Hall has been well preserved, complete with its original plasterwork and musicians' gallery. The Hall now displays a fine collection of paintings of local scenes, portraits and period photographs. The Regimental Museum of the Cameronians is on the same premises and its history is considered to be very much a part of the local scene. The Regiment was raised near Hamilton in 1689 and was disbanded in 1968. Since 1881 it had been in effect the County regiment. The Cameronians uniforms, medals, weapons

The Stable. Hamilton District Museum.

and other mementoes of nearly three hundred years of service to the Crown form a considerable collection. The Regimental Museum also includes an interesting group of relics of the Covenanters.

The display of horse-drawn vehicles includes a four-in-hand coach or drag, built in 1870 as the family coach of the Robertson-Aikmans of the Ross; a cabriolet; a dog-cart; a phaeton; a charabanc, built in 1895, which plied for excursion hire at Dunoon; a jaunting car; a fire engine of 1875; a superb late Victorian hearse; a hawker's float, and several other specialities.

The collection of motor cars is equally rich and comprehensive. The oldest example is Hamilton's first car, locally built in 1897, and there are a number of other vintage and veteran cars, mostly dating from the Twenties and Thirties. Like the horse-drawn vehicles, they have all been carefully restored and are in immaculate condition.

An excellent collection of harness, for road and farm use, is a most useful adjunct to the vehicles. Visitors are shown exactly how and where the different pieces fitted and the types of work for which they were designed. There are similarly attractive and practical exhibits of wheels and springs. The Museum is exceptionally well endowed with ploughs and with dairy equipment and these, too, are displayed in the Transport and Farm Equipment extension, together with a wide range of hand tools used in agriculture.

'We aim,' says the Curator, 'at displaying the local scene from the Bronze Age to the Twentieth Century', and although there is understandably a good deal more about the Victorians than about the Bronze Age, that is roughly what the visitor finds.

Auchindrain Museum of Country Life. *Auchindrain Museum Trust. Inveraray, Strathclyde. On the A83, south-west of Inveraray. Open Easter– September 30, M.–Sa. 10–6; Su. 2–6. Other months by appointment.*

Auchindrain is a very old settlement. It has been in the possession of the Campbells – Earls, Marquesses and Dukes – since that family's rise to power in the early 15th century. It was farmed as a communal-tenancy township until well into the present century, with the 18th and 19th century buildings still standing or identifiable. It once extended to several square miles of rough grazing, with small patches of arable ground, close to the township, but it now consists of about 20 acres of 'infield' and 23 18th and 19th century buildings in various states of repair.

In the 1950s, the Mid-Argyll Antiquarian Society, which was making a special study of Auchindrain, came to the conclusion that the township was well worth preserving as a whole. The Auchindrain Museum Trust was formed, to restore Auchindrain and to operate it as a folk museum. This has involved the reclamation and cropping of the arable ground, the rearing of appropriate livestock, the mounting of displays and exhibitions and the organisation of demonstrations.

Auchindrain avoided progress. Its ground was never divided into separate fields and it was farmed to provide a living for its inhabitants. From the area to which they had a right, the tenants had to provide themselves with food, shelter, fuel and clothes. They obtained extra income from time to time by casual work

with local industries – iron smelting, charcoal burning, fishing, quarrying.

The inhabitants of Auchindrain were self-reliant, independent people, who worked in real co-operation with one another. Some things they owned themselves and others they held in common. There was a communal bull – his shed is at present set up as a smithy – and a house, the 'puirhouse', specially built in the mid-19th century for a member of the community unable, for one reason or another, to earn enought to support himself. Two of the houses are furnished, one in the style of about 1850 and the other of 1890-1900. A barn built in the late 1820s now contains a display of barn and field implements.

The 'kailyards' were of great importance to the community, providing vegetables and certain soft fruits in season. They have been restored and planted to grow the traditional crops – kale, cabbage,

Stoner's House, Auchindrain Country Life Museum, Inveraray.

peas, beans, parsley, blackcurrants, redcurrants, and gooseberries. If the tenants had sufficient space, they often had damsons, plums and crab-apples as well. When the Trust took over the property, there was still a fine Victoria plum tree in front of one of the houses. The kail-yards were carefully protected by walls, but otherwise the animals were allowed to roam freely over the fields after the corn had been gathered, gleaning whatever they could in the way of food from them.

The Museum provides remarkable evidence of the hard work and resourcefulness that were needed to wring a living from the fields, hills and heather of Auchindrain. It is a microcosm of life as it once was over a large part of Scotland.

The Weaver's Cottage. *The National Trust for Scotland. Benvarran, Kilbarchan, Strathclyde. Open May 1–31 and September 1–October 31, Tu., Th., Sa., Su., 2–5. June 1–August 31, daily 2–5.*

Kilbarchan is associated with St. Barchan, one of the 6th century Irish missionaries who came to Renfrewshire. In medieval times it was a purely agricultural village of about 40 families. By the end of the 17th century some weaving was being done and the population had risen to nearly a thousand. Unlike the neighbouring textile town of Paisley, which paid the penalty of its over-specialisation in shawls and developed large factories, Kilbarchan, which had remained on a cottage basis, with the handlooms instead of the more intricate Jacquard looms, continued to weave textiles until the 1950s, although by that time only four looms were still working.

The Weaver's Cottage was built in 1723 and weaving continued in it until 1940. It was opened in 1957 as a memorial museum of the local weaving industry. Considerable restoration was necessary and the opportunity was taken to recreate something of the original character and atmosphere by suitable furnishing. The former living room and two smaller rooms originally contained box beds and these have been replaced. In the living room, the stone-flagged floor has been uncovered and many items of woodwork, pottery and metalwork with local associations have been introduced. These include appropriate fireside equipment, an oatcake roller and toaster, a peat oven and two cheese presses.

In a small room across the entrance passage are portraits of some of the last weavers of Kilbarchan and in another room beyond that are exhibits relating to the local weaving industry. There are examples of the tools used, among them a weaver's pocket glass for counting the number of threads per inch of fabric; samples of local fabrics – shirt patterns, tartans, and shawls. There was formerly a

An 18th century weaver's cottage. Kilbarchan.

weaving shop in the basement and this has been restored. It now includes two looms, one of which is in full working order.

In the garden visitors can see some-thing not often found nowadays – a recess in the wall known as a bee hole. This protected three of the old-fashioned type of circular bee skeps from the wind and rain.

The Highland Folk Museum. *Highland Regional Council. Duke Street, Kingussie, Highland. Open April 1–October 31, M.–Sa. 10–6; Su. 2–6, with evening openings M.–Sa. during July and August. November 1–March 31, M.–F. 10–3.*

The Highland Folk Museum has changed its home three times. Founded in 1934 by Dr. I.F. Grant, who had become a great enthusiast for folk museums after her visits to Northern Europe, it was first accommodated in the old United Free Church on Iona. From there the rapidly expanding Museum – Dr. Grant was a great collector – moved to a disused church in Lagan and then, in 1944, to Pitmain Lodge, a Georgian house at Kingussie, which had sufficient land to allow the kind of open-air museum Dr. Grant always had in mind. Between 1954, when Dr. Grant retired, and 1974, the Museum was owned and run jointly by the four ancient Scottish Universities – the

Agricultural Museum was added during this period – and it then passed complete-ly into public ownership, under the care of the Scottish Regional Council.

Dr. Grant envisaged the reconstruction of cottages at the Museum, to show local types of building and, in particular, to illustrate different stages in the evolution of the fireplace. Four buildings, not all of them houses, were in fact erected in her time – a dry-stone black house of the Lewis type, with no chimney, livestock under the same roof, and a 'ben' or good room, reserved for special occasions, like

The farming section. The Highland Folk Museum, Kingussie.

births, marriages and the laying out of the dead; a clack mill – a horizontal watermill of Norse type from the same area; a traditional Inverness-shire cottage; and an example of the 'improved' type of cottage encouraged by lairds throughout the Highlands in the latter part of the 19th century. These were all furnished from the collections and had sheep and cattle grazing round them. Unfortunately two of the houses were destroyed by fire, caused by sparks from steam railway engines running alongside the Museum property, and only the clack mill and the Lewis house remain to mark this stage of development.

As it now is, the Museum fulfils Dr. Grant's aim to showing something of the old Highland way of life, an intermingling of Pict, Celt and Viking into a society which depended heavily on its own resources. The collections, displayed in Pitmain Lodge, the adjoining MacRobert House and the long single-storeyed building specially constructed to show the farming collections, illustrate this, but also contain many reminders that Gaelic society was by no means cut off from the main stream of European culture. There are special displays of costume – fashionable early tartans and working clothes – domestic furnishings, and textile crafts, and a recently opened gallery contains country furniture from the 17th century to the 19th.

The Agricultural Museum shows objects in their working context, a stable, a barn, ploughing. The open-air museum now includes a Georgian shooting lodge and a special exhibition devoted to the Highland Tinker, including a tinker encampment with a four-wheeled waggon and displays of basketry, horn-working, silversmithing and other tinker crafts.

Souter Johnnie's Cottage. *The National Trust for Scotland. Kirkoswald, Ayrshire, on A77, 8 miles west of Maybole. Open April 1–September 30, Sa.– Th. 12–5. Other times by appointment.*

In 1775 Robert Burns was sent by his father to study mathematics at Hugh Rodger's school at Kirkoswald. He lodged with his uncle, Samuel Brown, who farmed close to Kirkoswald. During the months he spent there, Burns absorbed the material which he later used in his poem, *Tam O'Shanter*. He saw a great deal of Douglas Graham, tenant of the farm of Shanter, the prototype of Tam, having been introduced to him by the shoemaker, John Davidson, otherwise known as Souter Johnnie.

The Souter's cottage was built and occupied in 1785 by John Davidson. Before that, he had lived and worked at Glenfoot, near the farm of Shanter, and it was there at the farm that Burns got to know him first. On later visits to Kirkos-wald, however, he used to meet the Souter in the present cottage.

During the two centuries of its existence, the little thatched house has been modified internally from time to time to suit different occupants, the main change being the division into two separate dwellings, as evidenced by the two front doors, which have been allowed to remain. In the early 1920s it was taken over and restored by a local committee, formed for the purpose, and it subsequently passed into the possession of The National Trust for Scotland.

On the walls of the front room, which is open to visitors, are a number of old engravings of scenes from *Tam O'Shanter* and *The Cottar's Saturday Night*. Some items of 18th century furniture have also

Souter Johnnie's Cottage. Kirkoswald.

been placed in this room, together with the tools and equipment of a village cobbler of the period, among them a cobbling chair which was almost certainly used by the Souter. The kitchen, which is approached through the front room, still has its stone-flagged floor and old-fashioned open fireplace. There is a contemporary dresser, with a set of china cups and saucers and some plates which belonged to the Souter's grandmother, and various other items of domestic equipment used by the Souter's family. The two box beds preserve a character-

istic feature of the traditional Scots kitchen. The Souter died in one of them in 1808.

The garden behind the house was originally used to grow vegetables, especially potatoes. It is now a lawn, with four life-sized stone figures placed by the side of it in a group. They represent Tam O'Shanter, Souter Johnnie, the Innkeeper and his wife, and they were carved in 1802 by James Thom, a self-taught sculptor who was born in the village of Tarbolton, Ayrshire. They were exhibited in various towns in Scotland and England and, after remaining in private ownership for nearly a century, they were acquired for the cottage in 1924.

J.M. Barrie's Birthplace. *The National Trust for Scotland. 9 Brechin Road, Kirriemuir, Tayside. Open May 1–September 30, M.–Sa. 10–12.30, 2–6; Su. 2–6. Other times by appointment.*

James Barrie, author of *Peter Pan*, was born at Kirriemuir in 1860. His father was a handloom weaver. James was the second youngest of ten children and, when he was born, one of the downstairs rooms was still the workshop. Soon afterwards, the loom was moved into a nearby loom shop and the family had a sitting room for the first time.

Within a few years, factory production had taken over from the handloom weavers and, after a brief period as a bookkeeper in Forfar, David Barrie spent the rest of his days as Chief Clerk in the factory which had put him out of business. In 1870, after the Forfar interlude, the family rented a new villa in Kirriemuir and it was here that Barrie's mother and father died.

The house in Brechin Road in which J.M. Barrie spent the first eight years of his life had four rooms. In the late 1920s a report that it was to be taken down and re-erected as a Barrie Museum in the United States aroused considerable feeling in

The Parlour. J.M. Barrie's Birthplace, Kirriemuir.

Britain and in 1937, shortly after Barrie's death, it became the property of The National Trust for Scotland. Until 1961 it was let to Mrs. Betsy Thomson, who had known Barrie, and after her death in that year The National Trust restored the house as closely to its original appearance as possible, as a fitting memorial to one of Scotland's leading literary figures.

Since then, many personal possessions of the playwright and his family have been given to the Trust, and are on display in the Museum. They include two of the chairs for the future sitting-room that were carried into the house by his father on the day of Barrie's birth, the chair in which his mother nursed her children, the couch and settle from his London flat in Adelphi Terrace, Lavery's portrait of him and a number of manuscripts, letters, photographs and other memorabilia.

There are also Peter Pan jerkins, worn by two of the actresses who played the part, Pauline Chase and Jean Forbes-Robertson.

Linlithgow Canal Museum. *Linlithgow Union Canal Society. Canal House, Manse Road, Linlithgow, West Lothian. Open Easter–September 30, Sa., Su. 2–5.*

The Museum was opened in 1977, in the renovated stable built for barge horses by the side of the canal basin. An 80-year-old horse-drawn canal boat, the *Victoria*, is moored outside the Museum and provides canal trips on summer Saturdays and Sundays.

Planned and built at the end of the 18th

Linlithgow Canal Museum, Lothian.

210

LINLITHGOW CANAL MUSEUM

century to carry traffic between Falkirk and Edinburgh, a distance of 31 miles, the canal was a commercial success until the 1840s, with coal, stone and grain as the principal cargoes and good business with passengers as well. The railway was opened in 1842 and the canal gradually fell into disuse.

Since then, the Canal Society has concentrated its energies on promoting the canal as a place for recreation, rather than commerce. Apart from tidying up the surroundings of the waterway, its members have put sections of the tow path back into good condition, organised rallies and, not least, established the Museum. This now includes many original maps and documents concerning the building and operation of the Canal and an audio-visual display illustrates its history and the details of its route.

Considerable attention has been paid to the plants and wild creatures which can be found along the banks and tow path – a pleasant and civilised aspect of canal-going which is not usually in the enthusiast's repertoire. But both the Linlithgow Society and its Canal aim to cater for the people who want to do their exploring by water and those who prefer to do so on foot. So, as well as information about the navvies who dug the canal, the bargees who moved the boats along it, and aqueducts and the quantities of freight carried each year, we are offered lists of the natural exhibits to look for after leaving the Museum – the flowers that grow on the banks and on the edges of the tow paths, the marshland plants, the water plants, the trees and shrubs and the animals, birds and reptiles.

Everything has been achieved by voluntary effort and all the proceeds from the Museum and the boat trips go towards the restoration of the Canal and to making its attractions better known.

Opposite, above:
Souter Johnnie's Cottage figures, Kirkoswald, Strathclyde.

Opposite, below:
Mount Stewart House, Newtownards, Co. Down.

Following page, above:
Bunratty Castle and Folk Park, Co. Clare.

Following page, below:
Muckross House Folk Museum, Killarney, Co. Kerry.

Ulster

Fermanagh County Museum. *Fermanage District Council. Castle Barracks, Enniskillen, Co. Fermanagh. Open Tu.–Sa. 10–12.30, 2–5. Closed on July 12.*

The Museum is very attractively housed, along with the Museum of the Royal Inniskilling Fusiliers, in the Castle Keep at Enniskillen, a largely 17th century building which had been in a ruinous condition and which was excellently restored in the early 1960s. After a number of temporary exhibitions during 1977, the first stage of the permanent display was opened to the public in the summer of 1978. This illustrates the pre-history and early history of Fermanagh from the Middle Stone Age to the end of the Early Christian period. The story is told by means of archaeological material, much of it lent by the Ulster Museum and other museums, enlarged colour transparencies set in illuminated cases and three large-scale dioramas. One diorama shows a crannog, a man-made island settlement often found in Fermanagh, another a burial scene at one of Fermanagh's megalithic tombs, the Court Grave at Aghanaglack, and the third a scene in and around a rath or ring fort. These dioramas were designed by a local art teacher, Gordon Johnston, and their original style

Detail from a diorama of work on a dug-out canoe. Fermanagh County Musuem, Enniskillen.

has made a strong appeal to both adults and children.

This exhibition, to be followed soon by others which will bring the history of Fermanagh closer to our own times, uses the latest display techniques and yet manages to retain the atmosphere of a medieval castle. This has been achieved partly by skilful lighting, partly by

Fermanagh County Museum, Enniskillen, Co. Fermanagh.

modesty and restraint. It is a quiet museum, with no attempt to dazzle visitors with brilliant showmanship or to stun them with information. It possesses that rarest of all museum qualities, simple sophistication.

Ulster Folk Museum. *Trustees of Ulster Folk and Transport Museum. Cultra Manor, Holywood, Co. Down. Open May 1–September 30, M.–Sa. 11–7; Su. 2–7. Late opening, until 9 p.m. Tu. and W. only, in May and June. October 1–April 30, M.–Sa. 11–5; Su. 2–5.*

The Ulster Folk Museum occupies Cultra Manor and 70 acres of its estate. The remainder of the 136-acre site is parkland, interspersed with wooded glens. This makes a pleasant recreational area within the Museum complex. The Folk

Museum does not see itself merely as an assembly of objects. Its task, it believes, is to preserve and interpret ideas as well, to present a view of the traditional way of life in Ulster over the past two centuries and to suggest the way in which traditional

Ulster Folk Museum, Holywood, Co. Down.

Coach and Bicycle Gallery. Ulster Folk Museum, Holywood.

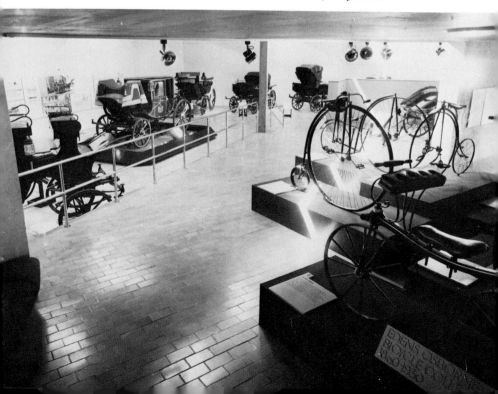

attitudes have been handed down to the people who are alive today.

The Museum is in two parts. Cultra Manor itself has been converted to form exhibition galleries, a reception centre and a museum shop. In these galleries, objects from traditional life are presented simply as objects, with little or no indication of the relationship between them. Relationships between objects can be seen and studied in the open-air folk park, which has buildings selected and removed from different parts of the Ulster countryside. These buildings illustrate not only the dwellings inhabited by ordinary people, but also their places of work. The aim is to help visitors, both from Northern Ireland and abroad, to understand how everything in the Museum once formed part of a complete way of life, which has now disappeared.

The living places – cottiers' houses, farmhouses, the home of well-to-do people from the Lough Neagh area – illustrate size, degree of comfort, building materials and domestic arrangements. They represent the private side of a person's life. The furniture, the fireplace, the pots and pans are not merely items from the past: they show how the housewife cooked, baked, tended the hearth, clothed her family, mended and managed and made a home.

The working places show the functions of people within the community. The weaver's house provides evidence of how families wove linen in their homes for sale to merchants at the town markets. The flax scutching mill has the water-powered machinery which extracted the fibres from the dried flax. The forge, built about 1830, is typical of the smithies which made everything of iron the community needed. The spade mill started operating in about 1840 and its massive water-driven hammer beat about a hundred different types of spade into rough shape. The old National School, built in 1836, was moved stone by stone to Cultra, complete with its desks and books. The parish church (1790) of Kilmore, Co. Down, arrived fully furnished, with its box pews.

The museum is growing all the time. The buildings already there will gradually be joined by others, representing a complete settlement pattern, illustrating both the open countryside, with its farms and mills, and a small village.

Mount Stewart House. *The National Trust. Co. Down, on the east shore of Strangford Lough, 5 miles south-west of Newtownards. Open April 1–September 30, Su.–Th. 2–6. Open Good Friday. Garden open April 1–October 31, 12–6.*

Mount Stewart, the property of the Marquesses of Londonderry, whose family name was Stewart, was built in the early 19th century. Much of the interior was redecorated and furnished a century later by Edith, Lady Londonderry, wife of the 7th Marquess, who also laid out the famous gardens surrounding the house. The gardens were given to the National Trust in 1957, the house, with many of its contents, twenty years later.

The house and estate reflect the wealth and taste of one of Ireland's most influential families and especially of Edith, Lady Londonderry. There are fine pieces of 17th, 18th and early 19th century furniture. They include the 22 chairs used by the delegates to the Congress of Vienna in 1815 and presented to Castlereagh's half-brother, Lord Stewart, at the conclusion of the Congress, as a memorial of the summit of both their diplomatic careers. Many items of furniture, as well as works of art, were brought to Mount Stewart from Londonderry House, the family's London house in Park Lane, which was demolished in the 1960s.

The large collection of paintings range from a Stubbs painting of the racehorse, *Hambletonian*, to the full-length portrait the Music Room of the first Lady Londonderry, shown with the harp she must have often played in this room. The porcelain includes, in addition to the Chinese and Meissen ware customary in such a house, some more out-of-the-way items, such as a noteworthy collection of porcelain vegetables and a small biscuit porcelain bust of Napoleon as a young man. One also discovers with pleasure several fine alabaster and marble urns and vases, which Edith, Lady Londonderry, had fitted with internal electric lighting, so that their beautiful translucency could be appreciated.

There are a number of homely touches among all the grandeur, such as the height of Lady Londonderry's children, marked, each birthday, on the wall of the two sets of doors leading to the Music room and, in the Entrance Hall, her needlework on many of the cushions, which bear the Londonderry cypher. It is the spirit of this remarkable woman, one of the last of the breed of great political hostesses, which is most marked at Mount Stewart.

The house has a number of associations with royalty. King Edward VII and Queen Alexandra stayed there in 1903, and before leaving they planted two copper beeches which still stand, opposite the north side of the house. In more recent years, King George VI and Queen Elizabeth were entertained at Mount Stewart, when they were Duke and Duchess of York.

Away from the house is the Temple of the Winds, built in the 1780s as a banqueting house. It has superb views across Strangford Lough and the family, with their guests and servants, were in the habit of spending days here during the summer months. When someone suggested to the 3rd Marquess that it would make an excellent mausoleum, he turned the idea down flat. 'I have', he wrote, 'no Taste for turning a Temple built for Mirth and Jollity into a Sepulchre. The place is solely appropriate for a Junketting Retreat in the Grounds.'

Opposite:
Breakfast Room. Mount Stewart House, Newtownards.

The Irish Republic

Bunratty Castle and Folk Park. *Shannon Free Airport Development Company. Bunratty, Co. Clare. Open daily 9.30–5.*

The present Bunratty Castle, completed in the middle of the 15th century, is the third to have been built at the point where the river at one time known as the Raite and now as the O'Garney joins the Shannon. The name Bunratty means 'the mouth of the Raite river'. Originally a stronghold of the O'Briens, Earls of Thomond, it eventually passed into the hands of the Studdert family. In 1956 it was sold to the late Viscount Gort, who helped the Office of Public Works to restore it and endow it with a collection of furniture, tapestries and works of art appropriate to the castle of a 16th or 17th century Irish nobleman.

The aim has been to make the furnishings match the scale and grandeur of the building and in this way to create an atmosphere which would recall Bunratty in its heyday. Few of the items are Irish – they are more likely to be French, Italian, Flemish, German or even English – and those who go to Bunratty expecting to find a notable collection of Irish furniture and Irish art are destined to be disappointed. So far as its contents are concerned, Bunratty belongs to Europe, rather than to Munster, but it is a splendid piece of theatre and a great deal more rewarding and enjoyable than the alternative, a bare shell of masonry, would be.

The Folk Park, established near the Castle, is an open-air museum, based on a collection of rural buildings – cottages, farmhouses, workshops – which have been brought from all parts of the Shannon region. The idea grew from the decision to save from annihilation a small farmhouse which stood in the way of runway extensions at Shannon Airport. Having rescued it, the new owners, the Shannon Free Airport Development Company, had to put it somewhere and

A 15th century panel from an altar piece depicting the story of St. Hubert. Bunratty Castle and Folk Park.

Bunratty was the answer. The Folk Park was opened in 1964 and it has continued to grow in size and popularity ever since.

Bunratty Castle and Bunratty Folk Park are now two of Ireland's largest tourist attractions and money spinners. At the height of the season they can be rather uncomfortably full, which is one of the almost inevitable marks of a successful museum nowadays, especially in a pleasant holiday area. Spring and autumn are the best times for Bunratty. One of the reasons for the remarkable popularity of the Folk Park is its liveliness. Things are always going on there – a blacksmith at work, butter being churned, a woman making soda bread in a pot oven over an open peat fire. This is social history, not for historians but for the ordinary tourist, including a good many from America and the Continent, and it is well done, good quality showmanship that keeps the right side of the sentimental and sees no harm in warmth and enthusiasm. A further extension is planned, to cover the social, political and economic life of yesterday's rural Ireland, and it will be extremely interesting to see how this potentially explosive commodity is served up for popular consumption.

Cobh Museum. *Cobh Museum Committee. Scots Church, High Road, Cobh, Co. Cork. May 1–September 30, Su. and W. 3–6. October 1–April 30, Su. 3–6. April 30, Su. 3–6.*

Cobh is a difficult place to classify. Built on the 10-acre Great Island in Cork Harbour, it is not really a port, a market town, a fishing town or an industrial town, yet it has something of the flavour and appearance of all four. It began life as a small fishing village, grew rapidly in the 18th century as a supply base for American convoys during the American War of Independence, saw the departure of hosts of emigrants during the 19th century and was described as 'the most fashionable bathing place in the south of Ireland'. It was a British and American naval base in World War I, a Port of Call for transatlantic shipping companies until the 1960s and is now a centre for container shipping and trawlers, steelworks,

Cobh Museum, Co. Cork.

shipyards and oil refining, with a thriving agricultural hinterland and still a population of no more than 6,000. Its little Museum has the formidable task of reflecting all this and it manages remarkably well.

The premises are sufficiently unusual to be helpful. The Museum is housed in the former 1954 Presbyterian Church, known as Scots Church. The number of Presbyterians in the area became fewer and fewer and in 1965 the Church was closed for public worship and given to Cork County Council 'for cultural purposes'. The County Council decided a museum for Cobh was the only cultural purpose in sight and the Museum opened its doors in 1973, in the knowledge that practically the only source of finance for the future was going to be voluntary subscription but that, on the other hand, Cobh was no ordinary place.

So, to hold the story together, there are two principal threads, a good series of historical records and pictures and a substantial collection of items dredged up from the harbour and ranging in time from the 18th century to nearly the present day. Nothing has been wasted, everything treasured, from the paten and chalice made for Scots Church to a rifle recovered from a German arms ship scuttled off Cobh in 1916, and from mementoes of the *Lusitania* disaster to a ring belonging to

Printing Press. Cobh Museum.

Edmund Burke, whose descendants providentially still live in the town.

In the best modern tradition, the Museum displays are presented as a springboard for exploring the district. 'The visitor,' he is told, 'may wish to see some places of special interest in the area, whose history is recalled by exhibits in the Museum' and then, armed with the Museum's extra-mural list, he is properly prepared to go exploring on his own.

Folk Village Museum. *Folk Village Trust. Glencolumbkille, Co. Donegal. Open Easter–September 30, daily 10–6.*

The Folk Village or Clachan in Glencolumbkille shows the development of Donegal's cottage dwellings over a period of three centuries. Traditionally, cottages were grouped in clusters, or clachans, to provide shelter, company and protection. The three which form the Museum here present living conditions as they were in

approximately 1720, 1820 and 1920. Each cottage has the traditional Donegal rounded thatch and contains original domestic equipment and furnishings of the period it represents.

The first cottage shows the relatively primitive living conditions of a cottier in 1720. The open fire has no chimney, there

is a beaten earth floor, settle and tester beds, a wooden 'cliabhan' or cradle and wooden vessels for eating and drinking, and a spinning wheel. Cooking, sleeping, eating, birth and death all take place in the one room.

By 1820 considerable improvements are noticeable. Life has become more convenient and comfortable. The chimney flue has appeared, flagstones provided a much better floor surface, the rush and tallow candles have been replaced by a single-wick paraffin lamp. A recess built into the kitchen wall accommodates an additional bed. There is a greater variety of kitchen utensils and plates, bowls and cups are made from pottery, not wood.

The cottage of 1920 is quite different from its predecessors. It is comparatively modern, even bourgeois, in arrangement and furnishing. There is a kitchen, bedroom and parlour, with plastered walls and, in the parlour, a coal-burning grate

Folk Village Museum, Glencolumbkille, Co. Donegal.

and ornament-loaded mantelpiece. Life in the clachan has changed its character.

The Museum was first established in 1966. Since then there have been a number of extensions and developments. A large new cottage has been built, in the traditional Donegal style, to display and sell Donegal handicrafts, and to provide additional exhibition space. The Museum now offers its visitors historical displays of Irish lace, household lamps from the rush candle to the Aladdin lamp, wooden vessels for holding milk and making butter, and country beds. There is also a comprehensive collection of the tools and equipment used to make Donegal tweed, from the time the wool leaves the sheep's back to the moment it comes off the loom.

Muckross House Folk Museum. *Trustees. Killarney, Co. Kerry, on road from Killarney to Kenmare. Open Easter–June 30 and September 1–October 31, daily 10–7. July 1–August 31, daily 9–9. November 1–Easter, Tu.–Su. 11–5.*

Muckross House was built in 1843 in an early Victorian version of the Tudor style for Henry Arthur Herbert, Member of Parliament for Co. Kerry, as his new mansion, the latest of a series of Herbert houses on the estate. The Portland stone used for the facings came by sea to Kenmare and then by cart over the mountains. There are 25 bedrooms in the main block, a large dining room, drawing room and library and elaborate domestic arrangements in the basement. The total cost of the building was only £30,000.

The Herbert family, who came to Kerry from Wales in Elizabethan times, owned the house until 1899 and in their time Muckross had 22 indoor servants. It was sold to Lord Ardilaun in 1899 and then in 1911 to William Bowers Bourn, who gave it to his daughter as a wedding present. In 1932 the house and estate of 11,000 acres was presented to the nation by the family.

A large part of the original furnishings and domestic equipment remain. The dining room in particular is much as it was when Queen Victoria and Prince Albert were guests in the house in 1861. There are many portraits, including one of Eugene Tagney, the Herberts' head gamekeeper, and another of the celebrated Countess of Desmond, who died in 1614, at a ripe old age, as the result of a fall from a cherry tree. The walls are decorated with trophies of the chase, hunting being an important feature of the life of the owners. In the front hall are the antlers of a giant Irish Deer, extinct for more than 10,000 years.

In different rooms and corridors of the house there are exhibits illustrating many aspects of Kerry and its history. These range from a collection of ferns found in the Killarney district to the Gaelic

Blacksmith. Muckross House Folk Museum. Killarney.

Athletic Association in Kerry. There are samples of different types of needlework, a flat square stone used as an altar in penal times, when the public practice of the Roman Catholic religion was virtually prohibited by law, and a representative selection of the birds and insects of Kerry.

The basement contains a series of displays which illustrate the trades and crafts of the past. There are agricultural implements, dairying equipment, carpenters', shoemakers', coopers' and wheelwrights' tools, the contents of a Killarney printing shop and examples of woodcarving and inlaying carried out in the Killarney area. The 19th century social and economic history of Kerry is told in terms of housing, with reconstructions of different types of houses indicated in the Censuses from 1821 to 1971. There is also a representation of a public house of the early years of the present century.

The Museum, which was established in 1964, has a policy of giving traditional craftsmen and their apprentices the opportunity of working at Muckross.

Weaving, blacksmithing and pottery are in operation at the moment and others are to be added shortly.

The extensive and beautiful gardens were first mentioned and highly praised in the 18th century. Many improvements were carried out by the last private owners, Mr. and Mrs. Arthur Vincent.

Rothe House Museum. *Kilkenny Archaeological Society. Parliament Street, Kilkenny, Co. Kilkenny. Open April·1–October 31, M.–Sa. 10.30–12.30, 3–5. All year round, Su. 3–5.*

This Elizabethan merchant's house built in 1594, was bought by Kilkenny Archaeological Society in 1966. It contains a museum of Kilkenny antiquities, a collection of period furniture, and the Society's library.

The Rothes came to Ireland from

Wales with the Norman invaders. They were prominent in public life in Kilkenny and became very wealthy towards the end of the 16th century. The family declined in influence during the 17th and 18th

Rothe House Museum.

centuries. For most of the Victorian period, Rothe House was used as a school and became somewhat decrepit. It is the only one remaining intact of many such stone houses built in Kilkenny at about the same period, and probably the only Tudor merchant's house left in Ireland. It consists, in fact, of three separate houses divided by paved courtyards. Communication between the houses is effected by a series of buildings on the north side of the courtyards.

Towards the end of the 19th century it was bought and restored by Timothy W. O'Hanrahan, an antiquarian and Gaelic enthusiast, who was a founder member of the Kilkenny branch of the Gaelic League, established to promote the revival of the Irish language. The League still has a base in Rothe House today.

The Museum that can be seen today is the second to have been installed in the building. The first, created by an earlier Archaeological Society, was moved to Dublin at the beginning of this century and is now in the National Museum. The second has been formed in recent years by the present Archaeological Society. It contains a variety of items of archaeological and historical interest, most of them found locally or presented by members of old Kilkenny families. There is a good collection of pewter, some stone axes and, in the second courtyard, a number of items of agricultural equipment.

The principal interest, however, is in the buildings themselves, which reflect the prosperous state of the town in Tudor and Jacobean times, and illustrate the kind of investment in property which a well-to-do family was able to make for itself. What eventually resulted was an elaborate complex of buildings, forming a Rothe enclave in the centre of the town. Each of the three houses was occupied by part of the family, with a mill, as communal brewhouse and a communal kitchen, the fireplace of which can still be seen. The original well, which provided water for the whole establishment, has been preserved. Its pedimented superstructure bears the date 1604.

Knock Folk Museum. *Custodians of Knock Shrine. Knock, Claremorris, Co. Mayo. Open May 1–October 31, daily 10–8.*

The Shrine at Knock is well on its way to receiving as many pilgrims as Lourdes. Its remarkable fame and popularity is due to the Apparition there, on 21st August 1879, at the south gable of the church, of Our Lady, St. Joseph and St. John the Evangelist. The Apparition was seen by fifteen people, all of whom were closely interrogated afterwards by the Church authorities. Their testimony was officially found 'trustworthy and satisfactory'.

By the 1970s, when the number of visitors both from Ireland and from overseas, had swollen to a torrent, it was felt that the range of attractions at Knock might be usefully extended. Many people had come long distances, and the opportunity to become better acquainted with Irish history and traditions was an addition to the pilgrimage which some at least of them would probably welcome. So the Folk Museum was created and opened to the public in 1973. The collections have grown steadily since then and a new building is being planned, in order to be able to display more of the items. This is no provincial establishment making the best of a few pieces of domestic equipment, ten dolls and a handful of agricultural implements. 'We are,' says the Curator, 'probably the best stocked museum in Ireland, excepting the

National Museum in Dublin'. One might perhaps add that Knock displays its collections a great deal better than the National Museum, starved of both funds and space.

Knock Folk Museum, Claremorris, Co. Mayo.

What the Folk Museum in fact does is to illustrate the economy and social life of rural Ireland at the time of the Apparition. In St. Joseph's Room the emphasis is on farming, peat gathering and the skilled trades. The Holy Family Room is a reconstruction of the traditional Irish living kitchen, the working, sitting and eating place of the house. The Room of Our Lady and the Lamb concentrated on the home and on domestic equipment and crafts, the Shrine Section and Archdeacon Cavanagh's Room deal with religious life as it was in the 1870s, the Room of the Witnesses is devoted to the fifteen witnesses of the Apparition, and St. John's Room to the Abbeys of Ireland. There is also a separately housed Agricultural Section and, that very Irish institution, the Car House, where the household kept its trap, or other form of horse-drawn vehicle for getting from place to place.

It is the portrait of a simple and, for the most part, contented society. 'The inhabitants of Knock,' the Museum tells us, 'were not very rich, nor were they very poor. There were some of them well-to-do, that is, living comfortably on their little farms. The most of them managed to grow enough potatoes for their families, which was their chief support. They grew oats, enough to pay the rent, and occasionally spared some to make a few hundreds of oatmeal for the summer season when potatoes were getting short or old. In the summertime it was very good diet to have stirabout and milk for breakfast; potatoes and milk and sometimes a few eggs and butter for dinner. This was for the middle classes of little farmers. A labouring man thought himself well-off if he could have a noggin of buttermilk with some potatoes for his dinner and perhaps was well satisfied if he had a plateful of flummery for supper.'

These were the people to whom the objects in the Museum belonged. They were the people who saw the Apparition.

Monaghan County Museum. *Monaghan County Council. The Courthouse, Monaghan, Co. Monaghan. Open Tu.–Sa. 10–1, 2–5. June 1–August 31, also Su. 2–5. Closed for public holidays and 'a period of around 10 days at Christmas'.*

Monaghan has the first and only County Museum Service in the Republic of Ireland. It is concerned with the archaeology, folklife and natural history of the county, an agreeable part of Ireland off the main tourist beat, which will assuredly return to favour once the troubles of neighbouring Ulster have come to an end.

County Monaghan had the full range of prehistoric settlements, Stone Age, Bronze Age and Iron Age, and the Museum has plenty of objects from all three, including a fine bronze cauldron from Lisdrumturk bog and a curious stone cup – or possibly lamp – found near Clontibret. From later settlements in the early historic and medieval periods there are many objects of everyday use, such as leather shoes, especially from the waterlogged crannogs of the County, where the peaty water has acted as a preservative.

There are at least twenty crannogs known in the County.

In the 17th century much of the land changed hands through war, sale and 'plantation' – the deliberate, controlled settlement of people considered by the British to be politically reliable. Large estates were created, agriculture was developed and towns grew up. In time, however, the new settlers became as dissatisfied with the Government as the natives had been and in the late 18th century many of them formed Volunteer Corps in an attempt to bring about social reforms. Badges of the local Corps are on display. The administration of County affairs was in the not very satisfactory hands of the Grand Jury up to the end of the 19th century. Some of the tableware belonging to this powerful body is on view.

As elsewhere in Ireland, the roads of Monaghan were abominably bad until recent times. The Ulster Canal was constructed in an effort to remedy the situation. It reached Monaghan by 1838 and Clones by 1840, but it was never a success, mainly because of a chronic shortage of water, especially in the County. The Museum exhibit relating to the Canal includes one of the milestones placed on the banks of the Canal. The Ulster Railway Company extended its line to Monaghan in 1858. The Company later became part of the Great Northern Railway and there are many evocative railway items on show.

Detail of 14th century medieval Cross of Clogher. Monaghan County Museum.

The best known crafts in Monaghan were lace and crochet-making. Lace was first made in Carrickmacross in about 1820, and the Museum has some good 19th century pieces. Carrickmacross lace is still made today by the sisters of St. Louis. Crochet-lace was made in Clones, where it became an important local industry. The items in the Museum include an elaborate collar and shoulder-piece. Apart from agriculture, however, the main industry in Monaghan was the manufacture of linen, which, like farming is well represented in the Museum's collections.

The local history section covers life in the five principal towns of the County, which has had more than its fair share of famine and hardship. The main themes here are religion, politics and sport, in something like that order of priority. There is a special display dealing with the Royal Irish Constabulary, the predecessors of the present Garda Siochana. Prominent among the exhibits is a constable's kit box, found in Monaghan Barracks during the hand-over of power to the new Irish Government in 1922.

The Irish Agricultural Museum. *The Irish Agricultural Museum (Johnstown Castle) Ltd. Johnstown Castle, Co. Wexford. 4 miles south-west of Wexford town. Open May 1–October 31, M.–F. 9–12.30, 1.30–5; Su. 2–5. Other times by appointment.*

Until 1978, Ireland was in the unenviable position of being the only country in Europe without an agricultural museum. For a nation whose economy depended heavily on farming, this was extraordinary

and, as many Irish people thought and said, disgraceful. However, as a result of

The Irish Agricultural Museum, Wexford, Co. Wexford.

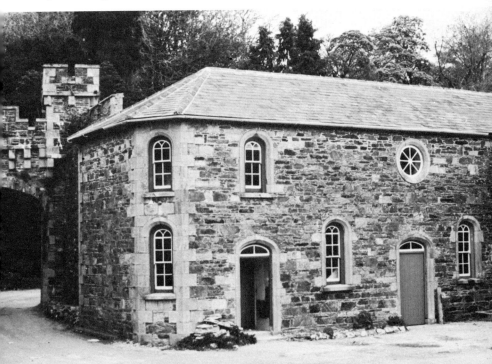

the hard work of a National Committee, the matter has now been put right and the new Museum enters its third season in 1980. The premises, made available by the Agricultural Institute, which is based close by, are ideal. The Johnstown Castle estate, which consists of 1,000 acres of farmland, woods, lakes and gardens, besides a large medieval castle, was presented to the nation in 1944 for use as an agricultural college. The fifty acres of ornamental gardens and lakes around the Castle have been open to the public free of charge since 1969, so that the new Museum has been established in a place which was already well-known and much visited. It has been installed in an attractive complex of restored farm buildings, dating from c.1820, grouped around a central courtyard.

The aim of the Committee was a simple one, 'to preserve and display Ireland's agricultural heritage', but the establishment of the Museum came at the eleventh hour, since in Ireland as elsewhere farming techniques and equipment have changed rapidly and radically during the past thirty years and much valuable museum material has been destroyed simply because nobody was looking out for it and because there was no home for it. However, farmers the world over are thrifty people, temperamentally disinclined to throw things away, just in case

they might come in useful some day, and maybe Irish farmers are thriftier than most, so that building up the basic collections has not been too difficult and, with museum agents busily at work all over the republic, new items are coming in all the time.

Each new season brings additions to the displays – this is a museum which certainly makes an annual visit very much worthwhile – but high among the present attractions are the restored and re-equipped harness room, the collection of farm machinery and the exhibits of dairy and animal management equipment. Reconstructions of craft workshops are being given a high priority in the list of future developments.

This, say its organisers, is a museum 'where we ourselves and future generations can go and see the methods and implements which served our ancestors well, where we can get the feel of the triumphs, the hardships, the inventiveness, the dogged perseverance and sheer hard work of those past generations which moulded the landscape into what we know today'. These things are very quickly forgotten and Johnstown is a good place to remember just how poor a country Ireland has been in the past and how desperately hard its people have had to work in order to survive.

Maps

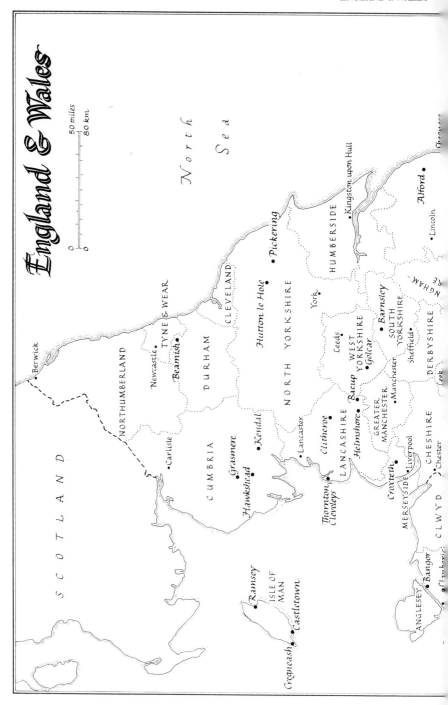

England & Wales

50 miles
80 km

0
0

North Sea

SCOTLAND

Berwick

NORTHUMBERLAND

Newcastle
Beamish

TYNE & WEAR

DURHAM

Carlisle

CUMBRIA

Grasmere

Hawkshead

Kendal

Thornton
Cleveleys

Lancaster

Clitheroe

LANCASHIRE

Helmshore
Croston

Bacup

GREATER
MANCHESTER

Manchester

Liverpool

MERSEYSIDE

Chester

CHESHIRE

CLWYD

ANGLESEY

Bangor

Ramsey

ISLE OF
MAN

Castletown

Cregneash

Hutton le Hole

CLEVELAND

Pickering

NORTH YORKSHIRE

York

Leeds

WEST
YORKSHIRE

Golcar

Sheffield

SOUTH
YORKSHIRE

Barnsley

DERBYSHIRE

HUMBERSIDE

Kingston upon Hull

Lincoln

Alford

NGHAM

RE

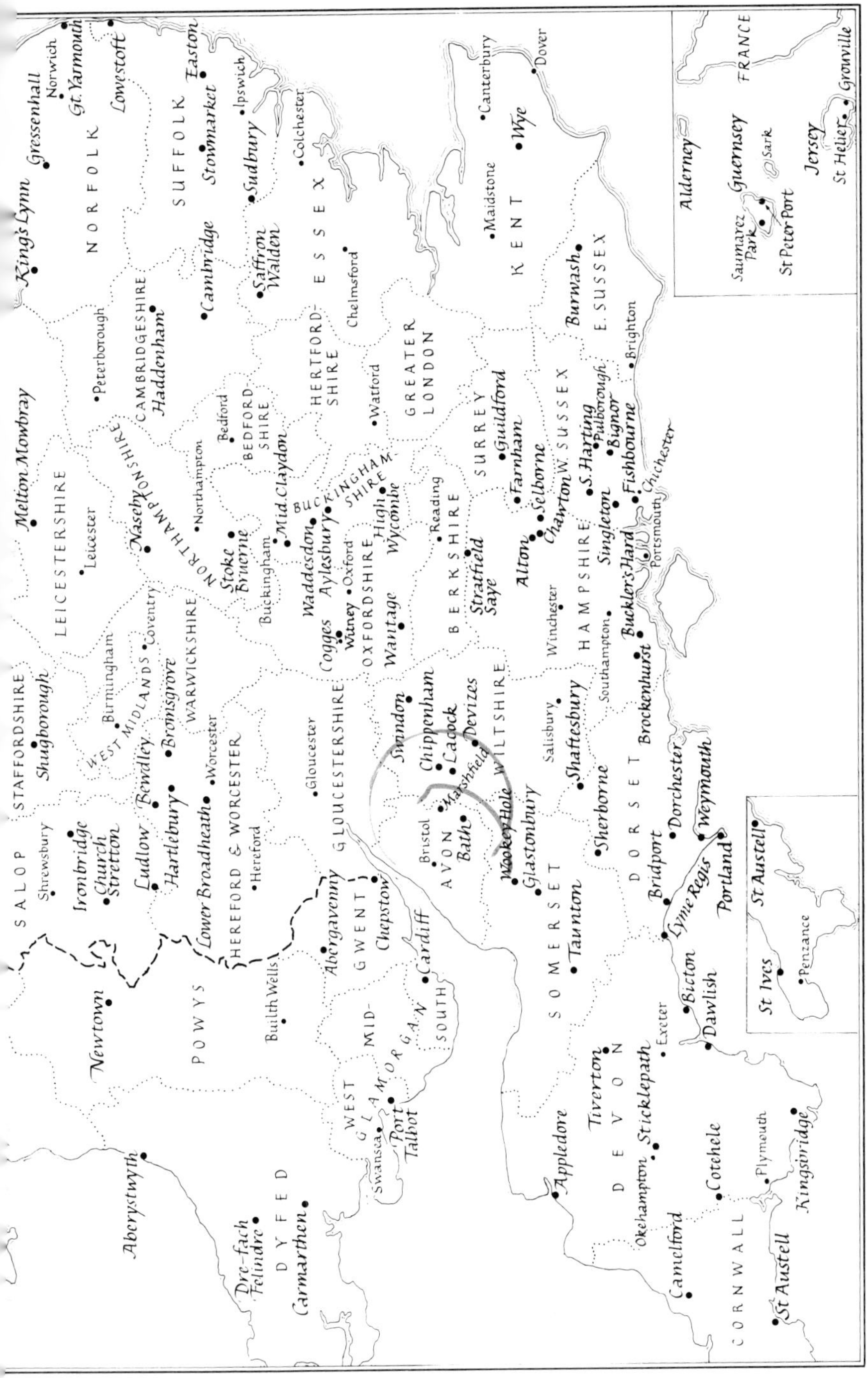

FRANCE

Alderney

Saumarez Park Guernsey
St Peter Port Sark
Jersey
St Helier Granville

Dover
Canterbury
Wye
Maidstone
KENT

Norwich
Gt. Yarmouth
Lowestoft
Easton
Kings Lynn Gressenhall
NORFOLK
Stowmarket Ipswich
SUFFOLK
Sudbury Colchester
Cambridge
ESSEX
Saffron Walden Chelmsford
Haddenham
CAMBRIDGESHIRE
Peterborough
HERTFORD-SHIRE
Watford
GREATER LONDON
Bedford
BEDFORD-SHIRE
SURREY
Guildford
Melton Mowbray Shugborough
LEICESTERSHIRE
Leicester
NASEBY SHIRE NORTHAMPTON SHIRE
Northampton
Stoke Bruerne
Buckingham
BUCKINGHAM-SHIRE
Waddesdon
Aylesbury Mid Claydon
Coventry
WARWICKSHIRE
Coges Witney Oxford
OXFORDSHIRE
High Wycombe
Reading
BERKSHIRE
Wantage
Farnham
Selborne
Alton
Stratfield Saye
Winchester
HAMPSHIRE
Southampton
Crawton W. SUSSEX S. Harting
Singleton Tilburough Bignor
Bucklers Hard Fishbourne
Portsmouth Chichester
Burwash
E. SUSSEX
Brighton

STAFFORDSHIRE
SALOP
Shrewsbury
Ironbridge Church Stretton
Ludlow Bewdley Bromsgrove
Hartlebury
WEST MIDLANDS
Birmingham
Worcester
Lower Broadheath
HEREFORD & WORCESTER
Hereford
GLOUCESTERSHIRE
Gloucester
Swindon
Chippenham
Lacock
Marshfield Devizes
WILTSHIRE
Salisbury
Shaftesbury
Sherborne
DORSET
Bridport Dorchester
Weymouth
Lyme Regis Portland
St Austell

POWYS
Newtown
Builth Wells
Abergavenny
GWENT
Chepstow
Cardiff
SOUTH
MID-
WEST
GLAMORGAN
Swansea Port Talbot
Aberystwyth
Dre-fach Felindre
DYFED
Carmarthen
Bristol
AVON
Bath
Wookey Hole
Glastonbury
SOMERSET
Taunton

St Ives
Penzance
St Austell
CORNWALL

Camelford
Cotehele
Plymouth
Kingsbridge
Okehampton Sticklepath
Exeter
DEVON
Tiverton
Bicton
Dawlish
Appledore

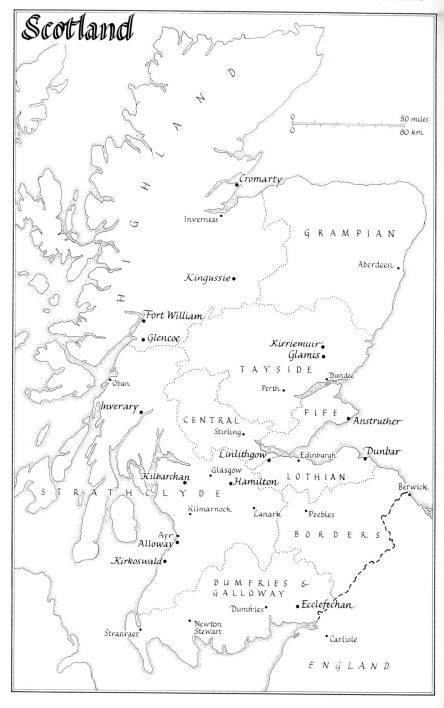

Scotland

50 miles
0
0
80 km

H I G H L A N D

Cromarty

Inverness

G R A M P I A N

Aberdeen

Kingussie

Fort William

Glencoe

Kirriemuir
Glamis

T A Y S I D E

Oban

Dundee

Perth

Inverary

F I F E

C E N T R A L

Anstruther

Stirling

Linlithgow

Edinburgh

Dunbar

Glasgow

Kilbarchan

Hamilton

L O T H I A N

S T R A T H C L Y D E

Berwick

Kilmarnock

Lanark

Peebles

B O R D E R S

Ayr
Alloway

Kirkoswald

D U M F R I E S &
G A L L O W A Y

Ecclefechan

Dumfries

Stranraer

Newton
Stewart

Carlisle

E N G L A N D

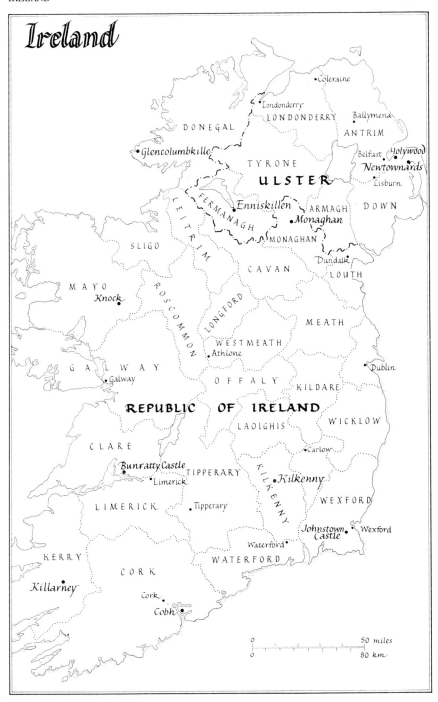

Index